# Be prepared...
# To learn...
# To succeed...

Get **REA**dy. It all starts here. REA's preparation for the NJ ASK is **fully aligned** with the Core Curriculum Content Standards adopted by the New Jersey Department of Education.

*Visit us online at*
***www.rea.com***

# READY, SET, GO!®

# NJ ASK
## Mathematics
## Grade 6

**With REA's TestWare® on CD-ROM**

**Steven T. Flanders**
Woodland Hills High School
Pittsburgh, Pennsylvania

**Todd P. Campanella**
Crockett Middle School
Hamilton Township, New Jersey

*Research & Education Association*
www.rea.com

The Performance Standards in this book were created and implemented by the New Jersey State Department of Education. For further information, visit the Department of Education website at *www.state.nj.us/njded/cccs*.


**Research & Education Association**
61 Ethel Road West
Piscataway, New Jersey 08854
E-mail: info@rea.com


*Ready, Set, Go!*®
**New Jersey ASK Mathematics Grade 6
with TestWare® on CD-ROM**


**Published 2013**

Copyright © 2010 by Research & Education Association, Inc. All rights reserved. No part of this book may be reproduced in any form without permission of the publisher.

Printed in the United States of America

Library of Congress Control Number 2009937719

ISBN-13: 978-0-7386-0557-9
ISBN-10: 0-7386-0557-3

REA®, *Ready, Set, Go!*®, and TestWare® are registered trademarks of Research & Education Association, Inc.

# Contents

## UNIT I:   Number and Numerical Operations

# UNIT IV: Data Analysis, Probability, and Discrete Mathematics

# About Research & Education Association

Founded in 1959, Research & Education Association (REA) is dedicated to publishing the finest and most effective educational materials—including software, study guides, and test preps—for students in elementary school, middle school, high school, college, graduate school, and beyond.

Today REA's wide-ranging catalog is a leading resource for teachers, students, and professionals.

We invite you to visit us at *www.rea.com* to find out how "REA is making the world smarter."

# Acknowledgments

We would like to thank REA's Larry B. Kling, Vice President, Editorial, for supervising development; Pam Weston, Vice President, Publishing, for setting the quality standards for production integrity  and managing the publication to completion; John Cording, Vice President, Technology, for coordinating the design and development of REA's TestWare®; Diane Goldschmidt, Senior Editor, for project management, editorial guidance, and preflight editorial review; Senior Editors Alice Leonard and Kathleen Casey, for post-production quality assurance; Heena Patel, Technology Project Manager, for design contributions and software testing efforts; Rachel DiMatteo, Graphic Artist, for her design contributions; and Christine Saul, Senior Graphic Designer, for cover design.

We also gratefully acknowledge the writers, educators, and editors of REA for content development, editorial guidance, and final review. Thanks to S4Carlisle for page design and typesetting.

# About the Authors

**Steven T. Flanders** is a calculus teacher at Woodland Hills High School in Pittsburgh, Pennsylvania. He has a Master's degree in Curriculum and Instruction from Gannon University and is currently pursuing his Doctor of Education Degree in Mathematics Education from the University of Pittsburgh. He is an expert in preparing students for standardized tests and has demonstrated success with urban students on both the Pennsylvania State System of Assessment (PSSA) Tests and the Advanced Placement Calculus AB and BC exams.

**Todd P. Campanella** is a middle school mathematics teacher at Crockett Middle School in Hamilton Township, New Jersey. Mr. Campanella specializes in preparing students for the NJ ASK Mathematics tests both in his classroom and through his company, TPC Math Tutors LLC, which provides in-home tutors and solution assistance throughout New Jersey.

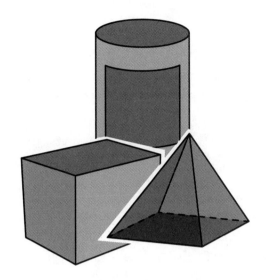

# Introduction

## About This Book and Testware®

This book, along with REA's exclusive TestWare® software, provides excellent preparation for the New Jersey ASK6 Mathematics test. Inside, you will find lessons, drills, strategies, and practice tests—all with a single-minded focus: success on the NJ ASK6, an acronym that stands for Assessment of Skills and Knowledge.

We have made every effort to make the book easy to read and navigate. The practice tests are included in two formats: in this book and software package. **We recommend that you begin your preparation by first taking the practice exams on your computer.** The software provides timed conditions and instantaneous, accurate scoring that makes it easier to pinpoint your strengths and weaknesses.

## Students

This book was specially written and designed to make test practice easy and fruitful for you. Our practice tests are very much like the actual NJ ASK tests, and our review is filled with illustrations, drills, exercises, and practice questions to help you become familiar with the testing environment and to retain information about key topics.

## Parents

The NJ ASK and other state assessment tests are designed to give you and the school personnel information about how well children are achieving in the areas required by New Jersey's Core Curriculum Content Standards, which describe what students should know at the end of certain grades. This book helps your children review and prepare effectively and positively for the NJ ASK in Mathematics.

### *Teachers*

Because you introduce students to the test-taking environment and the demands of the NJ ASK tests, our authoritative book can help you develop planned, guided instruction and practice testing. Effective preparation means better test scores!

## What Is the NJ ASK?

The New Jersey Assessment of Skills and Knowledge is a standards-based assessment used in New Jersey's public schools. Performance on the NJ ASK test does not equate with the grades students receive for teacher-assigned work, but rather with proficiency measures pegged to how well students are acquiring the knowledge and skills outlined in the state's Core Curriculum Content Standards. Those proficiency measures fall into three broad categories, or bands: "partially proficient," "proficient," and "advanced proficient."

## When Is the NJ ASK Given?

The test is administered in early spring. Grade 6 students take the NJ ASK Mathematics test over two days in early May. During each session, students are asked to complete a combination of multiple-choice questions and open-ended questions. Total testing time is about two hours, which does not include the time used for distributing and collecting materials and reading directions.

## What Is the Format of the NJ ASK?

The NJ ASK has two types of questions: multiple-choice and open-ended. The multiple-choice questions require students to choose the correct answer out of four possible choices and fill-in the appropriate circle in their answer booklet. The open-ended questions require students to write written responses in their own words. Each test section is timed, and students may not proceed to the next section until time for the current section has expired. If students have not finished a section when time runs out, they must stop and put down their pencils. There are clear directions throughout the test.

Students will be allowed to use a calculator on some sections of the test. In addition, a reference sheet showing important formulas and information will be provided to the test takers. There is no need for the students to memorize the formulas and information. If any other materials (such as a protractor or ruler) are necessary for taking the test, they will be provided to the students.

## Topics Covered on the NJ ASK6

There are five standards covered on the NJ ASK Grade 6 Mathematics test. Listed below are the standards and their associated strands.

Number and Numerical Operations

    A. Number Sense

    B. Numerical Operations

    C. Estimation

Geometry and Measurement

    A. Geometric Properties

    B. Transforming Shapes

    C. Coordinate Geometry

    D. Units of Measurement

    E. Measuring Geometric Objects

Patterns, Algebra, and Functions

    A. Patterns

    B. Functions and Relationships

    C. Modeling

    D. Procedures

Data Analysis, Probability, and Discrete Mathematics

    A. Data Analysis (Statistics)

    B. Probability

    C. Discrete Mathematics—Systematic Listing and Counting

    D. Discrete Mathematics—Vertex-Edge Graphs and Algorithms

Mathematical Processes

    A. Problem Solving

    B. Communication

C.   Connections

D.   Reasoning

E.   Representations

F.   Technology

## How to Use This Book and TestWare®

The best way to prepare for a test is to practice, and you'll find that we've included drills with answers throughout the book, and that our two practice tests include detailed answers.  You'll find that our practice tests are very much like the actual ASK6 you'll encounter on test day.

To make the most of your study time, we suggest that you take practice test 1 on CD-ROM to determine your strengths and weaknesses, and then study the course review material, focusing on your specific problem areas. The course review includes the information you need to know when taking the test. Make sure to follow up by taking practice test 2 on CD-ROM so you're thoroughly familiar with the format and feel of the NJ ASK6 Mathematics test.

## Test Accommodations and Special Situations

Every effort is made to provide a level playing field for students with disabilities who are taking the NJ ASK. Most students with educational disabilities and most students whose English language skills are limited take the standard NJ ASK. Students with disabilities will be working toward achieving the standards at whatever level is appropriate for them. Supports such as large-print type are available for students who have a current Individualized Education Program (IEP) or who have plans required under Section 504 or who use these supports and accommodations during other classroom testing.

If the IEP team decides that a student will not take the NJ ASK in Language Arts Literacy, Mathematics, and/or Science, the child will take the Alternate Proficiency Assessment (APA).

## Format and Scoring of the NJ ASK6 Mathematics Test

The questions on the NJ ASK can contain items/and concepts learned in earlier grades, covered by the Mathematical Processes standard.

The NJ ASK Mathematics test for Grade 6 contains a total of 44 test items. Thirty-five of these items are multiple-choice, six items are short constructed-response questions and three items are extended constructed-response items. Calculators may be used on all sections of the text except for the short constructed-responses.

Each multiple-choice question is worth 1 point. Short constructed-response questions are each worth 1 point and the extended constructed-response items are worth 3 points each. The highest score a student can receive on the Mathematics portion of the NJ ASK 6 is 50. Multiple-choice questions are scored by machine.

In addition to the basic test outline listed above, the New Jersey Department of Education also includes field test content in the NJ ASK Grade 6 Mathematics test. These items are not identified and are not scored. Students should do their best to answer all the questions on the test, as there is no way of knowing which items are field-test items and which are not. The practice tests in this book do not include field-test items.

## Where Can I Obtain More Information About the NJ ASK?

For more information about the NJ ASK, contact the State Department of Education or Educational Testing Service:

Office of Evaluation and Assessment
New Jersey Department of Education
PO Box 500
Trenton, NJ 08625-0500
Telephone: 609-292-4469

Or visit these helpful websites:

www.state.nj.us/education
www.ets.org/njask

## Tips for Test Taking

- **Do your homework.** From the first assignment of the year, organize the day so there is always time to study and keep up with homework.
- **Communicate.** If there are any questions, doubts or concerns about anything relating to school, study, or tests, speak up. This goes for teachers and parents, as well as students.
- **Get some rest.** Getting a good night's sleep before the test is essential to waking up sharp and focused.

- **Eat right.** Having a good breakfast—nothing very heavy—the morning of the test is what the body and mind need. Comfortable clothes, plenty of time to get to school, and the confidence of having prepared properly are needed by every student.

- **Test smart.** Listen carefully and follow all directions. Read the questions carefully. Make sure answers are written correctly in the proper place on the answer sheet. Don't rush, and don't go too slowly. If there is time, go back and check questions that you weren't sure about.

- **Eliminate incorrect answers.** Using you reasoning and estimating skills, eliminate all answers that cannot possibly be correct. You'll increase your chances of choosing the correct answer if you can eliminate one or two incorrect answers.

- **Think.** On the open-ended questions on the test, you are being scored on your ability to explain mathematics, not on how well you write a sentence. Use the mathematical symbols and expressions you know.

- **Be confident.** You will do your best if you think with confidence.

# Unit I
## Number and Numerical Operations

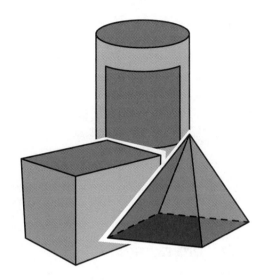

# Chapter 1
# Number Sense

## Place Value—Comparing Whole Numbers and Decimals

When comparing and reading whole numbers and decimals, it is useful to use a place-value chart.

| Hundreds | Tens | Ones | . | Tenths | Hundredths | Thousandths |
|----------|------|------|---|--------|------------|-------------|
|          |      |      | . |        |            |             |

When reading a decimal number, the number is read from the left to the right. The decimal point is read as "and," not point. The place value of the digit farthest to the right is read at the end of the decimal.

**Examples 1-3**  **Write the following decimal numbers and whole numbers in words.**

1.  16 is written as _____ .

## Solution:

16 is written as <u>sixteen</u>.

2. 10.31 is written as ___ten___ and ___thirty-one___ hundredths.

## Solution:

10.31 is written as ten and thirty-one hundredths.

3. 103.092 is written as ___one hundred three and ninety-two thousandths___

## Solution:

103.092 is written as <u>one-hundred three and ninety-two thousandths</u>.

---

**Examples 4-6**    Write the number for each word name:

4. One hundred thirty-two and fourteen thousandths _____

## Solution:

One hundred thirty-two and fourteen-thousandths is the number 132.014.

5. Ten and nine-hundredths _____

## Solution:

Ten and nine-hundredths is the number <u>10.09</u>.

6. One thousand three and eight-tenths _____

## Solution:

One thousand three and eight-tenths is the number <u>1,003.8</u>.

---

**Example 7**    Jacob walked through the museum and saw that the length of the average centipede is 7.096 centimeters. What should Jacob say when his teacher asks him how long is the centipede?

## Solution:

Step 1:   Write the number correctly in the place-value chart.

| Hundreds | Tens | Ones | , | Tenths | Hundredths | Thousandths |
|----------|------|------|---|--------|------------|-------------|
|          |      | 7    | . | 0      | 9          | 6           |

Step 2:   Write the decimal number.

7.096 is written as seven and ninety-six thousandths.

Decimals can also be represented as parts of a whole. Write the decimal that represents the shaded portion of the region. _____

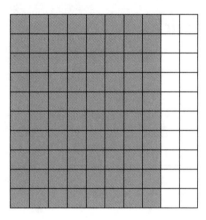

**Solution:** 0.80 is eighty hundredths.

Two decimals that represent the same amount are called *equivalent decimals*.

**Example 8**   **What is an equivalent decimal to 0.80?**

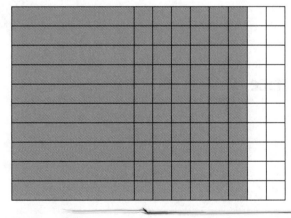
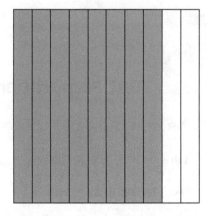

0.80 = 0.8

Eighty hundredths is equivalent to _____

## Solution:

Eighty hundredths is equivalent to <u>eight-tenths</u>.

## Lesson Practice

Write the name of the number in words.

1.   8.9 _eight and nine-tenths_

2.   0.675 _six hundred seventy-five thousandths_

3.   1003.004 _one thousand three and four-thousandths_

Write the number for each word name.

4.   twelve and forty-two hundredths _12.42_

5.   one hundred ninety-six and eleven thousandths _196.011_

6.   fourteen hundredths _0.14_

Fill in the blank with the word that makes the sentence true.

7.   fifteen and four _hundredths_ = fifteen and forty thousandths

8.   six and sixty thousandths = six and _six-hundredths_

## Test Preparation Practice

Circle the letter of the best answer.

1.   Which of the following is true?

A.   Six-tenths = 0.06

B.   Eleven-hundredths = 0.11

C.   Eleven-thousandths = 0.11

D.   Six-tenths = 0.006

2.  Which word name correctly describes 123.62?

    A.  One hundred and twenty-three and sixty-two hundredths

    B.  One hundred twenty-three and sixty-two thousandths

    C.  One hundred twenty-three and sixty-two hundredths

    D.  One twenty-three and sixty-two hundredths

3.  Which place value correctly describes the underlined digit: 2,3<u>1</u>4.91?

    A.  Hundreds

    B.  Tens

    C.  Ones

    D.  Tenths

4.  Which of the following could describe the shaded region?

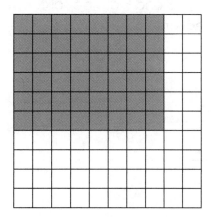

    A.  4.8

    B.  0.048

    C.  forty-eight

    D.  forty-eight hundredths

5.  Jamie bought a used car for one thousand nine hundred ninety-nine dollars and ninety-five cents. Which number below represents that amount?

    A.  $1,999.99

    B.  $1,995.99

    C.  $1,999.95

    D.  $1,959.95

## Whole Numbers and Integers

The whole numbers represent the set of numbers 0, 1, 2, 3, 4, ....

The integers are all of the whole numbers and the negative whole numbers.

..., −3, −2, −1, 0, 1, 2, 3, ...

To compare integers, we often use a number line.

The numbers to the right of zero are called positive numbers. The numbers to the left of zero are called negative numbers. Zero is neither positive nor negative.

Two numbers that are the same distance from zero in opposite directions are called opposites. For example, −3 and 3 are opposites because they are both 3 units from zero, but in opposite directions.

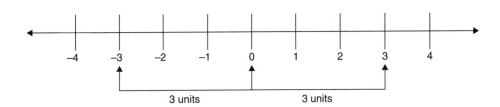

| Example 1 | **List six negative numbers.** |

## Solution:

−1, −3, −4, −7, −10, −11 (answers may vary)

| Example 2 | **What is the opposite of −14?** |

## Solution: 14

Integers can be used to model real-life events and situations.

**Example 3**    The coldest desert on Earth is the Dry Valleys of Antarctica, where temperatures can drop to eighty-nine degrees below zero Celsius. Write the number that represents how cold it gets in the Dry Valleys of Antarctica.

**Solution:**  $-89°$ C

## Lesson Practice

Write the integer that the situation describes.

$\checkmark (a + b)$

1.  He grew six inches taller. ___6___

2.  The sub sank two-hundred feet below sea level. ___−200___ ✓

3.  Stan lost thirty-five dollars when his wallet was stolen. Marsh
    ___−35___ ✓

4.  Jill's savings account earned her three dollars of interest. ___3___ ✓

5.  The bank charged Sam's checking account a one dollar ATM fee.
    ___−1___ ✓

6.  Mount Everest is twenty-nine thousand twenty-nine feet above sea level. What is the opposite of Mount Everest's height? ___−29,029___ ✓

## Test Preparation Practice

Circle the letter of the best answer.

1.  Which integer best represents the following situation? The football team lost ten yards because of a holding penalty.

    A.  10

    B.  0

    C.  −10

    D.  −0

2. Which situation does the integer 4 represent?

   A. Spending four dollars on candy

   B. Buying four remote control cars

   C. The temperature decreasing four degrees

   D. A withdrawal of four dollars from your bank account

3. Which number does the arrow point to on the number line?

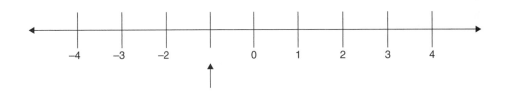

   A. 1

   B. −1

   C. −0

   D. 0

4. Choose the statement that is true

   A. The opposite of zero is zero

   B. Zero is a positive number

   C. Zero is a negative number

   D. None of these statements are true

## Comparing Whole Numbers, Integers, and Decimals

To compare numbers, we use three symbols:
    Greater than (>),
    Less than (<),
and
    Equal to (=).
    A helpful way to compare numbers is to write the numbers on a number line.

| **Example 1** | **Use a number line to fill-in the following sentence with >, <, or =.** |

11.7 _____ 12.2

## Solution:

Since 11.7 is left of 12.2, we say that 11.7 is less than 12.2.
11.7 __<__ 12.2

| **Example 2** | **Use a number line to fill-in the following sentence with >, <, or =.** |

−6.7 _____ −6.3

Since −6.7 is left of −6.3, we say that −6.7 is less than −6.3.
−6.7 __<__ −6.3

**Example 3**    **Use the table below to answer the following questions.**

| Career Batting Averages of Famous Baseball Players | |
| --- | --- |
| **Baseball Player** | **Career Batting Average** |
| Babe Ruth | 0.342 |
| Barry Bonds | 0.298 |
| Alex Rodriguez | 0.307 |

1.  Which player has the highest career batting average?

## Solution:

Babe Ruth, since 0.342 > 0.307 > 0.298

2.  Which player has the lowest career batting average?

## Solution:

Barry Bonds, since 0.298 < 0.307 < 0.342

3.  On the number line, mark where each batting average would fall.

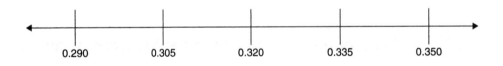

## Solution:

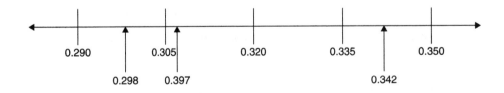

## Lesson Practice

Compare the numbers. Write >, <, or = to write a true statement.

1. −6.023 __>__ −6.139

2. −11.145 __<__ −11

3. 1.75 __>__ 1.705

4. 1,098,323 __<__ 1,980,323

5. 3,476.777 __<__ 3,476.877

6. 34.67 __=__ 34.670

Write a decimal number in the blank that makes the statement true.

7. 1.3 = __1.30__ < __1.31__

8. −1.67 < __−1__ < −0.5

9. 2.04 < __2.3__ < 2.40

10. −2.7 > __−2.71__ > −2.79

## Test Preparation Practice

Circle the letter of the best answer.

1. Which of the following statements is false?

    A. −6.08 < −6.0

    **B.** 17.17 = 17.017

    C. 2.1 < 2.19

    D. 3.6 > 3.19

2. The table below lists several football teams and the amount of money they charge per ticket.

| Team Name | Cost of Ticket |
|---|---|
| New York | $68.50 |
| Los Angeles | $59.95 |
| Atlanta | $59.50 |
| Philadelphia | $60.00 |

Which of the following lists shows the ticket prices from cheapest to most expensive?

A. New York, Los Angeles, Atlanta, Philadelphia

B. New York, Philadelphia, Atlanta, Los Angeles

C. Los Angeles, Atlanta, Philadelphia, New York

D. Atlanta, Los Angles, Philadelphia, New York

3. Jack bought a used car for $3,250.00. Jill bought a used car for $1,999.99. Jane bought a used car that costs less than Jack's car but more than Jill's car. Which price below may be how much Jane's car costs?

A. $4,000.00

B. $1,000.00

C. $200.00

D. $2,000.00

4. Which number would make the following sentence true?

$$-3.12 < \_\_\_\_ < -2.6$$

A. $-2.06$

B. $2.7$

C. $-3.5$

D. $-3.02$

5.  How many integers lie between −1.96 and 2.35?

   A.  One

   B.  Two

   C.  Three

   D. Four

## Open-Ended Questions with Whole Numbers, Integers, and Decimals

When giving written responses, make sure to show all your work and if the directions ask you to explain why you did something, make sure you do so.

**Example 1**    **In a golf tournament, the lowest score wins. Five players competed in a golf tournament and the scores of the first four players were 73, 75, 70, and 69.**

i)   What score would be necessary for the fifth player to finish fourth?

ii)  If the fifth player wins the tournament, what is the highest score he could have posted?

iii) If the fifth player finishes last, what is the lowest score he could have posted?

## Solution:

   Step 1:   Put the scores in order from lowest to highest: 69, 70, 73, 75
   Step 2:   Answer all parts of the question.

i)   What score is necessary for the fifth player to finish fourth?
     Answer:  We are looking for a number that fits between 73 and 75. Thus, the answer is 74.

ii)  If the fifth player wins the tournament, what is the highest score he could have posted?
     Answer:  Since winning the tournament means posting the lowest score, we want to know the highest number that would still be lower than the other four numbers. In this case, 68.

iii) If the fifth player finishes last, what is the lowest score he could have posted?
   Answer:  Since finishing last means that he posted the highest score, we
             want to know the lowest number that is greater than all of the other
             scores. In this case, 76.

## Lesson Practice

1.  The following table presents the daily highs and lows for the temperature in
    degrees Fahrenheit during a one-week period.

| Day | High | Low |
| --- | --- | --- |
| Monday | 83 | 49 |
| Tuesday | 96.7 | 56.1 |
| Wednesday | 79.03 | 55.92 |
| Thursday | 68.67 | 50.02 |
| Friday | 80 | 55 |
| Saturday | 79.34 | 61 |
| Sunday | 90.3 | 55 |

a)  Which day was the hottest of the week? _Tuesday was the hottest day._

b)  Write a statement that compares the daily highs for Wednesday
    and Thursday. _The high on Wednesday was higher than the highest
    temperature on Thursday._

c)  Arrange the days from coldest to hottest by comparing the low temperature
    for each day. _Monday, Thursday, Friday, Sunday, Wednesday, Tuesday,
    Saturday_

## Test Preparation Practice

1.  At the Olympics, five gymnasts had the following scores:

    8.7, 9.05, 9.12, 8.75, 9.32

    Use the following clues to determine which gymnast had which score.

    Let A, B, C, D, and E represent the gymnasts.

    a)  $D < B < E$

    b)  $C < A < E$

    c)  $D < A < E$

    d)  $B < C < A$

    Gymnast A = ___9.12___ ✓

    Gymnast B = ___8.75___

    Gymnast C = ___9.05___

    Gymnast D = ___8.7___

    Gymnast E = ___9.32___

    Explain how you know your answer is correct.

    My answers fit in with all the requirements (a), b), c), d)). A-8.7<8.75<9.32, B-9.05<9.12<9.32, C-8.7<9.12< 9.32, D-8.75<9.05 <9.12 ✓

 # Chapter 1—Solutions

## Place Value—Comparing Whole Numbers and Decimals

### Lesson Practice

1. eight and nine-tenths
2. six hundred seventy-five thousandths
3. one thousand three and four-thousandths
4. 12.42
5. 196.011
6. 0.14
7. Hundredths
8. six-hundredths

### Test Preparation Practice

1. B
2. C. Choice A is incorrect because the word "and" should not appear to the left of the decimal point.
3. B
4. D
5. C

## Whole Numbers and Integers

### Lesson Practice

1. +6
2. −200
3. −35
4. +3
5. −1
6. −29,029

### Test Preparation Practice

1. C
2. B
3. B
4. D

## Comparing Whole Numbers, Integers, and Decimals

### Lesson Practice

1. >
2. <
3. >
4. <
5. <
6. =
7. 1.30 < 1.35, answers may vary
8. −1, answers may vary
9. 2.10, answers may vary
10. −2.71, answers may vary

### Test Preparation Practice

1. B
2. D
3. D
4. D
5. D

## Open-Ended Questions with Whole Numbers, Integers, and Decimals

### Lesson Practice

1. a) Tuesday
   b) Wednesday's high is greater than Thursday's high
   c) Monday, Thursday, Friday, Sunday, Wednesday, Tuesday, Saturday

### Test Preparation Practice

1. Gymnast A = 9.12
   Gymnast B = 8.75
   Gymnast C = 9.05
   Gymnast D = 8.7
   Gymnast E = 9.32

By putting all of the clues together, we get the string of inequalities D < B < C < A < E.

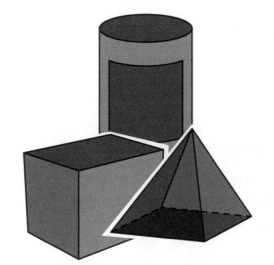

# Chapter 2 Using Numerical Operations on Whole Numbers, Integers, and Decimals

## Adding and Subtracting Decimals

To add or subtract decimals, first, line up the decimal points, then add or subtract the digits in the same place-value rows.

**Example 1**    Find the sum of 32.23 and 6.79

### Solution:

First, line up the decimal points:

```
   32.23
+   6.79
─────────
   39.02
```
Then, add the digits in the same place-value rows.

| **Example 2** | Find the difference of 16.5 and 11.97 |

## Solution:

First, line up the decimal points.

$$\begin{array}{r} 16.5\underline{0} \\ -\ 11.97 \\ \hline 4.53 \end{array}$$

Then, subtract the digits in the same place-value rows.

Since there were not the same amount of digits in the first number as the second, we needed to write in a zero in the hundredths place of the first number.

| **Example 3** | If Patrick pays $60.00 to buy a pair of sneakers that cost $54.78, how much change will he receive? |

## Solution:

$$\begin{array}{r} \$60.00 \\ -\ \$54.78 \\ \hline \$\ 5.22 \end{array}$$

is the amount of change that Patrick will receive.

| **Example 4** | The table below shows the distances in meters that several athletes jumped in the long jump at a recent track meet. |

a) How much farther did the winner jump than the person who finished in third place?

b) What was the total distance jumped by all the athletes?

| Results from the Long Jump ||
| --- | --- |
| **Athlete** | **Distance (m)** |
| Kyle James | 6.72 |
| Jake Smiley | 7.09 |
| David Eason | 6.4 |

## Solutions:

a)　　7.09
　　− 6.4<u>0</u>

　　　0.69 m　　Thus, the winner jumped 0.69 m farther than the third place winner jumped.

b)　The total distance jumped is the sum of the distances. Thus,

　　　6.72
　　　7.09
　　+ 6.4<u>0</u>

　　　20.21 m jumped.

---

| **Example 5** | **Claudia buys a purse for $9.99 and gets her haircut for $29.79.** |
|---|---|

a)　How much did Claudia pay for both her purse and her haircut?

b)　How much money should Claudia have left over if she started with $50.00?

## Solutions:

a)　　$29.79
　　+ $ 9.99

　　　$39.78 is the cost of the total purchase.

b)　　$50.00
　　− $39.78

　　　$10.22 is the money Claudia should have left over after shopping.

## Lesson Practice

For questions 1–4, add or subtract the decimals.

1.  $5.2 + 3.6 =$ ___8.8___ ✓
2.  $9.78 - 6.03 =$ ___3.75___ ✓
3.  $11.75 + 0.53 =$ ___12.28___ ✓
4.  $1.267 - 1.08 =$ ___0.187___ ✓

Use the table below to answer questions 5–7.

Rebekah counted her change in her piggy bank and found she had the following amounts of money in quarters, dimes, nickels, and pennies.

| Money in Coins | |
|---|---|
| **Coin** | **Amount of Money** |
| Quarters | $3.75 |
| Dimes | $2.50 |
| Nickels | $0.85 |
| Pennies | $0.56 |

5.  How much more money does Rebekah have in dimes than in nickels?
    ___$1.65___ ✓

6.  How much money does Rebekah have in total of both nickels and pennies?
    ___$1.41___ ✓

7.  How much money does Rebekah have? ___$7.66___ ✓

8. How much change should Courtney receive if she gave the cashier $40.00 to purchase a CD set that costs $33.69? In words, describe what steps you took to solve the problem.

   *$6.31, I subtracted $33.69 from the $40.00 Courtney gave. The leftover of $6.31 was the change.*

9. If an amusement park requires customers to be 48 inches tall to ride a roller coaster, how many more inches does a person who is 41.73 inches tall need to grow? _*6.27 Inches.*_ ✓

## Test Preparation Practice

Circle the letter of the best answer.

1. Jason buys shoes for $59.99 and a shirt for $19.49. If he pays with a $100.00 dollar bill, how much change should he receive?

   A. $20.52

   B. $59.50

   C. $35.96

   D. None of the above

2. If you had $46.75 in your savings account at the start of the month and then withdrew $25.00 and then deposited $6.95, how much money would now be in your savings account?

   A. $78.70

   B. $59.80

   C. $28.70

   D. None of the above

3. The distance Steve walked each morning for the past four days is listed in the table below.

| Day | Distance (miles) |
|---|---|
| Monday | 4.2 |
| Tuesday | 3.9 |
| Wednesday | 4.45 |
| Thursday | 4.05 |

Which of the following statements is false?

A. Steve walked further on Monday and Tuesday than he did on Wednesday and Thursday.

B. Steve walked further on Tuesday and Wednesday than he did on Monday and Thursday.

C. The total distance that Steve walked is greater than 15 miles.

D. Steve walked further on Monday than he did on Thursday.

## Multiplication and Division of Whole Numbers

Often, we have to use multiplication and division to solve problems that occur in real life situations.

When multiplying two numbers, the numbers that we multiply are called factors. The answer to a multiplication problem is called the product.

**Example 1** Eagle Elementary School expects to use 654 sheets of paper per student this coming year. If there are currently 79 students enrolled at Eagle Elementary School, how much paper does the school need?

## Solution:

To multiply by two-digit numbers, we multiply the first factor by each number in the two digit factor and then add the two products.

$$654 \times 79 =$$

Step 1:  Multiply 654 by the 9 in the ones column of the second factor.

$$654 \times 9 = 5{,}886$$

Step 2:  Multiply 654 by the 7 in the tens column of the second factor. (Remember that a 7 in the tens column really represents 70, thus we place a zero in the ones column as a placeholder.)

$$654 \times 70 = 45{,}780$$

Step 3:  Add the two products together.

$$654 \times 79 = 5{,}886 + 45{,}780 = 51{,}666$$

Step 4:  State the answer.

Eagle Elementary School will need 51,666 sheets of paper.

We typically use division to solve problems when we want to know how many individual items make up a group, or when we wish to separate many individuals into groups. When using division to solve problems, the number that we divide is called the dividend, the number that we divide by is known as the divisor, and the answer to a division problem is called the quotient.

**Example 2**    **Find the quotient of 465 and 9.**

## Solution:

To solve a long division problem, follow these steps: compare and divide, multiply, subtract and bring down, then repeat.

Step 1:  Compare and Divide.

$$\begin{array}{r} 5 \\ 9\overline{)465} \end{array}$$

Compare the divisor (9) with the first digit of the dividend (4). Since $9 > 4$, we cannot divide. So, we compare the divisor with the first two digits of the dividend. Since $9 < 46$, we can divide. We ask ourselves, how many times can 9 go into 46? We place the answer to that question, 5, in the tens place in the quotient.

Step 2:  Multiply the number in the quotient by the divisor and write the product under the dividend.

$$\begin{array}{r} 5 \\ 9\overline{)465} \\ 45 \end{array}$$, since $5 \times 9 = 45$.

Step 3:   Subtract the product from the dividend and then bring down the next
digit in the dividend.

$$
\begin{array}{r}
5\phantom{00} \\
9{\overline{\smash{\big)}\,465\phantom{0}}} \\
-\ 45\downarrow\phantom{0} \\
\hline
15\phantom{0}
\end{array}
$$
, 46 − 45 = 1, then bring down the 5.

Step 4:   Repeat.

$$
\begin{array}{r}
51\phantom{0} \\
9{\overline{\smash{\big)}\,465\phantom{0}}} \\
-\ 45\downarrow\phantom{0} \\
\hline
15\phantom{0} \\
-\ \phantom{0}9\phantom{0} \\
\hline
6\phantom{0}
\end{array}
$$

Divide 9 into 15, write a 1 in the ones place of the quotient, then multiply the 1 by
the 9 and write the product beneath the 15. Subtract the 9 from the 15. When there
are no further digits in the dividend to bring down, the answer to the subtraction
problem is called the remainder.

$$
\begin{array}{r}
51\text{R}6 \\
9{\overline{\smash{\big)}\,465\phantom{0}}} \\
-\ 45\downarrow\phantom{0} \\
\hline
15\phantom{0} \\
-\ \phantom{0}9\phantom{0} \\
\hline
6\phantom{0}
\end{array}
$$

**Example 3**   **What is 953 divided by 54?**

## Solution:

$$
\begin{array}{r}
17\text{R}35 \\
54{\overline{\smash{\big)}\,953\phantom{0}}} \\
-\ \phantom{0}54\downarrow\phantom{0} \\
\hline
413\phantom{0} \\
-\ 378\phantom{0} \\
\hline
35\phantom{0}
\end{array}
$$

**Example 4**    If six 2-liter bottles of soda cost a total of $18.00, how much does one 2-liter bottle of soda cost?

## Solution:

This is an example of a problem that requires separating a group (the six 2-liter bottles) into individual items (one 2-liter bottle). So, we will use division.

Since we want to know the cost of one bottle, we will divide the total cost by the total number of bottles. $18.00 ÷ 6 = 3. Thus, the cost of one 2-liter bottle of soda is $3.00.

## Lesson Practice

For questions 1–4, find the product.

1.  36 × 14 _____504_____
2.  718 × 34 _____24,412_____
3.  504 × 123 _____61,992_____
4.  1,592 × 408 _____649,536_____

For questions 5–8, find the quotient and remainder.

5.  614 ÷ 31 _____19 R25_____
6.  1,897 ÷ 15 _____126 R7_____
7.  45)960 _____21 R15_____
8.  7)607 _____86 R5_____

9.  On a trip from New York City to Los Angeles, a family drove 3,000 miles and used 86 gallons of gas. How many miles did they drive on one gallon of gas during this trip? _____About 35 MPG_____

10.  If one CD at the music store costs $12.99, how much will 3 CDs cost?
    _____$38.97_____

## Test Preparation Practice

Circle the letter of the best answer.

1.  If Team A spends $20.00 per player and has 12 players, and Team B spends $18.00 per player and has 14 players, which team spends more money?

    A.  Team A

    B.  Team B

    C.  They spend the same amount of money

    D.  Not enough information

2.  A dairy farm milks 150 cows per day. The total amount of milk produced after a milking is 975 gallons of milk. How much milk does one cow produce?

    A.  146,250 gallons

    B.  0.154 gallons

    C.  6.5 gallons

    D.  65 gallons

3.  A parking garage has enough space for 650 cars. The cost per car is a flat rate of $20.00 per car. Which of the following could be the total amount of money collected by the parking garage?

    A.  $8,200

    B.  $15,000

    C.  $6,550

    D.  $15.00

4.  A bag of chocolate candies is separated into equal groups of 5 pieces and given to 11 children. After the candy is given out, 4 pieces of candy are left over. How much candy was in the bag originally?

    A.  5 pieces

    B.  55 pieces

    C.  51 pieces

    D.  59 pieces

## Multiplication and Division of Decimals

Multiplying and dividing decimals is very useful when solving problems involving money and many other everyday situations.

When multiplying decimals, multiply as you would if the numbers were whole numbers. To determine where to place the decimal point in the product, add the number of decimal places in the factors. The number of decimal places in the product will be the same as the sum of the decimal places in the factors.

**Example 1**    **Multiply 4.75 × .62.**

**Solution:**

$$
\begin{array}{r}
4.75 \\
\times\ 0.62 \\
\hline
950 \\
+\ 2850 \\
\hline
29450
\end{array}
$$

To determine where to place the decimal point in the answer, add the number of decimal places in the factors. 2 + 2 = 4. Thus, place the decimal point after 4 digits in the product. So, the answer is,

$$
\begin{array}{r}
4.75 \\
\times\ 0.62 \\
\hline
950 \\
+\ 2850 \\
\hline
2.9450
\end{array}
$$

**Example 2**    **Find the product of 0.405 and 1.02.**

**Solution:**

$$
\begin{array}{r}
0.405 \\
\times\ 1.02 \\
\hline
0810 \\
0000 \\
+\ 0405 \\
\hline
0.41310
\end{array}
$$

**Example 3**  If the price of a gallon of milk is $3.43 per gallon, how much does it cost to buy 8 gallons of milk?

## Solution:

Multiply the price of one gallon of milk times 8 gallons.

$$
\begin{array}{r}
3.43 \\
\times \quad 8 \\
\hline
27.44
\end{array}
$$

Eight gallons of milk will cost $27.44.

To divide decimals, we must multiply both the divisor and dividend by the same power of ten. We choose the power of ten by deciding how many places we need to move the decimal point so that the divisor becomes a whole number.

**Example 4**  What power of ten should you multiply the divisor and dividend by to divide 3.675 by 0.43?

## Solution:

Since 0.43 is the divisor, we need to multiply it by 100, so that the divisor will become 43. The dividend will also be multiplied by 100 and will become 367.5.

**Example 5**  Divide 33.6 by 2.75.

## Solution:

$$2.75 \overline{)33.6}$$

To find the quotient, we must first multiply both the divisor and the dividend by 100 in order to make the divisor a whole number.

$$2.75 \times 100 = 275, \qquad 33.6 \times 100 = 3360$$

$$
\begin{array}{r}
12\text{R}60 \\
275 \overline{)3360} \\
-\ 275 \\
\hline
610 \\
-\ 550 \\
\hline
60
\end{array}
$$

**Example 6**    An airplane flies from Newark International Airport to Paris, France. If the flight lasts for 9.25 hours and the distance from Newark to Paris is 5,000 miles, how many miles per hour does the plane fly?

## Solution:

We need to divide the distance of the flight by the time necessary to make the flight.

$5000 \div 9.25 = 9.25\overline{)5000}$

$$
\begin{array}{r}
540 \text{ R}500 \\
925\overline{)500000} \\
-\ 4625 \phantom{00} \\
\hline
3750 \phantom{0} \\
-\ 3700 \phantom{0} \\
\hline
500 \\
-\ \ 0 \\
\hline
500
\end{array}
$$

Thus, the speed of the plane is about 540 miles per hour.

## Lesson Practice

For questions 1–4, find the product.

1.  $2.65 \times 3.5$  __9.275__ ✓

2.  $1.089 \times .45$  __0.49005__ ✓

3.  $0.041 \times 1.67$  __0.06847__ ✓

4.  $112.3 \times 9.04$  __1,015,192__ ✓

For questions 5–8, find the quotient.

5.  $2.6\overline{).89}$  __0.342 (about)__ ✓ (0.34)

6.  $0.78\overline{)2.04}$  __2.03 (about)__ ✗ 2.615

7. 8.13)‾10.1‾   _1.24 (about)_ ✓   (1.242)

8. 0.0403)‾0.11101‾   _2.51 (about)_ ✗ 2.7546

9. If a watermelon weighs 3.2 pounds and costs $6.24, how much does the watermelon cost per pound?   _$1.95 per pound_ ✓

10. Grapes are on special at the grocery store, where 1 pound of grapes costs $0.89. How much does 2.5 pounds of grapes cost?   _$2.23_ ✓

## Test Preparation Practice

Circle the letter of the best answer.

1. One United States dollar is worth eight Guatemalan Quetzals. How many Guatemalan Quetzals is 3.5 United States dollars worth?

   (A.) 28

   B. 2.286

   C. 0.4375

   D. None of the above

2. The area of a rectangle is the product of the length and the height. What is the area of a rectangle whose length is 14.25 inches and whose height is 5.75 inches?

   A. 2.478 square inches

   (B.) 81.94 square inches

   C. 0.404 square inches

   D. None of the above

3. Steve has a lawn mowing business. He charges $22.50 per hour to mow lawns. If his total income last week was $348.75, how many hours did he mow?

   A. 15

   B. 0.155

   C. 1.55

   (D.) 15.5

4.  The area of a rectangle is found by multiplying the length of the rectangle by the width of the rectangle. If the area of a rectangle 16.525 square inches, and its length is 8.105 inches, how wide is the rectangle?

    A.  20.39 inches

    B.  2.039 inches

    C.  13.39 inches

    D.  133.9 inches

## Finding Squares and Cubes of Whole Numbers

To find the square of a number, you multiply the number by itself.

For example, $1 \times 1 = 1$. Thus, 1 is a square number and can be written as $1^2 = 1$. Some other common square numbers are listed below:

$2^2 = 2 \times 2 = 4$
$3^2 = 3 \times 3 = 9$
$4^2 = 4 \times 4 = 16$

To find the cube of a number, the number must be multiplied by itself three times. For example, $1 \times 1 \times 1 = 1$. Thus, 1 is a cube number and can be written as $1^3 = 1$. Some other common cube numbers are listed below:

$2^3 = 2 \times 2 \times 2 = 8$
$3^3 = 3 \times 3 \times 3 = 27$
$4^3 = 4 \times 4 \times 4 = 64$

| Exponent Form | Read in Words | Multiplication Form | Value |
|---|---|---|---|
| $5^2$ | Five squared, or five to the second power | $5 \times 5$ | 25 |
| $5^3$ | Five cubed, or five to the third power | $5 \times 5 \times 5$ | 125 |

Often, geometric models are used to represent square and cube numbers.

For example, $2^2$ or "two squared" can be geometrically represented by drawing a two-by-two square.

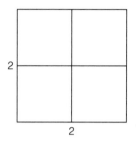

$$2^2 = 2 \times 2 = 4$$

Similarly, we can draw cube numbers in a similar manner.

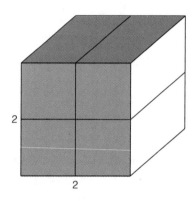

$$2^3 = 2 \times 2 \times 2 = 8$$

| Example 1 | Write $6^3$ in multiplication form. |

## Solution:

$6^3 = 6 \times 6 \times 6$

| Example 2 | Evaluate $7^3$. |

## Solution:

$7^3 = 7 \times 7 \times 7 = 49 \times 7 = 343$

| Example 3 | What is nine cubed? |

## Solution:

Nine cubed is $9^3 = 9 \times 9 \times 9 = 81 \times 9 = 729$

**Example 4**    Draw a model that represents $6^2$.

## Solution: 6

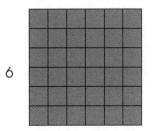

6

## Lesson Practice

1.  Write $4^3$ in multiplication form. _4x4x4_
2.  What is $8^2$? _64_
3.  Which is smaller, $7^2$ or $4^3$? _$7^2$_

## Test Preparation Practice

Circle the letter of the correct answer.

1.  Which expression is the same as $6^3$?

    A.  $6 \times 3$

    B.  $3 \times 3 \times 3 \times 3 \times 3 \times 3$

    C.  $6 \times 6 \times 6$

    D.  $3 \times 6$

2. Fill in the blank with the appropriate inequality symbol: $2^3$ ___ $3^2$.

   A. =

   B. >

   C. <

   D. None of the above

3. Which of the following is not a cube number?

   A. 125

   B. 64

   C. 27

   D. 81

# Order of Operations Involving Addition, Subtraction, Multiplication, Division, and Parentheses

When we evaluate numerical expressions involving a combination of numbers and operations, the order of operations tells you in which order to solve the problem. The order of operations can be remembered by the acronym, PEMDAS.

Parentheses
Exponents
Multiplication and Division
Addition and Subtraction

First, evaluate any expression within parentheses, or some other grouping symbol.

Second, find the value of all powers.

Third, multiply and divide in order from left to right.

Last, add or subtract in order from left to right.

**Example 1**   **Find the value of the expression.**

$5 + 4 \times 7$

## Solution:

$5 + 4 \times 7 = 5 + 28$, multiply 4 and 7, first
       $= 33$, add 5 and 28.

**Example 2**    Evaluate: $2 \cdot 4^2 - 10 + 6$

## Solution:

$2 \cdot 4^2 - 10 + 6$
$= 2 \cdot 16 - 10 + 6$ , evaluate $4^2$
$= 32 - 10 + 6$ , multiply 2 and 16
$= 22 + 6$ , subtract $32 - 10$
$= 28$ , add $22 + 6$.

**Example 3**    Four people go to the movies and two of them buy popcorn. If a movie ticket costs $7.50 and a bag of popcorn costs $3.75, how much was the total bill?

## Solution:

To find the total cost, we must first write an expression and then evaluate it. The total cost is the cost of the tickets plus the cost of the popcorn.

Cost of the tickets = 4 × $7.50        since four people bought a movie ticket at $7.50 per ticket

Cost of the popcorn = 2 × $3.75        since two people bought popcorn at $3.75 per bag of popcorn.

Total Cost = 4 × $7.50 + 2 × $3.75 = $30.00 + $7.50 = $37.50
The total cost of the trip to the movies is $37.50.

## Lesson Practice

For questions 1–4, evaluate the expression.

1.  $(7 - 2) \times 6 + 3$ _____ 45  ×33

2.  $36 \div (3 + 9) - 2 + 5$ _____ 6

3.  $64 \div (-4) + 25 \div 5^2$ _____ −15

4.  $(15 - 7) \div 4 + 3^2$ _____ 11

5.  At a high school baseball game, student tickets cost $4 per ticket. All other tickets cost $6 per ticket. How much would admission cost for a group of three students and six guests? _____ $48

## Test Preparation Practice

Circle the letter of the best answer.

1. Evaluate the expression $4 + 3 \times 5 - 10$.

   A. 25

   B. 9

   C. 2

   D. 20

2. What is 50 plus 14 divided by 7 minus 10?

   A. 19

   B. 42

   C. 36

   D. 11

3. Which expression equals 8?

   A. $(10 - 4) + 4^2 \div 2 - 6$

   B. $10 - (4 + 4^2) \div 2 - 6$

   C. $7 \times 10 - 9 + 1$

   D. $7 \times 10 - (9 + 1)$

4. Which expression represents 8 times the sum of 6 and 4 divided by 12?

   A. $8 \cdot 6 + 4 \div 12$

   B. $8 \cdot 6 - 4 \div 12$

   C. $8 \cdot (6 + 4) \div 12$

   D. $8 \cdot (6 - 4) \div 12$

5. If macaroni salad costs $4 per pound and potato salad costs $2.50 per pound, what is the total cost of 3 pounds of macaroni salad and 4 pounds of potato salad?

   A. $23.50

   (B) $22.00

   C. $13.50

   D. $120.00

# Chapter 2—Solutions

## Adding and Subtracting Decimals

### Lesson Practice

1. 8.8
2. 3.75
3. 12.28
4. 0.187
5. $1.65
6. $1.41
7. $7.66
8. $6.31. You should subtract the cost of the CD from the money given to the cashier. $40.00 − $33.69 = $6.31.
9. 6.27

### Test Preparation Practice

1. A
2. C
3. A

## Multiplication and Division of Whole Numbers

### Lesson Practice

1. 504
2. 24,412
3. 61,992
4. 649,536
5. 19R25
6. 126R7
7. 21R15
8. 86R5
9. 34.88 miles
10. $38.97

### Test Preparation Practice

1. B
2. C
3. A
4. D

## Multiplication and Division of Decimals

### Lesson Practice

1. 9.275
2. 0.49005
3. 0.06847
4. 1,015.192
5. 0.34
6. 2.615
7. 1.242
8. 2.7546
9. $1.95 per pound
10. $2.23

### Test Preparation Practice

1. A
2. B
3. D
4. B

## Finding Squares and Cubes of Whole Numbers

### Lesson Practice

1. $4 \times 4 \times 4$
2. 64
3. $7^2$

### Test Preparation Practice

1. C
2. C
3. D

## Order of Operations Involving Addition, Subtraction, Multiplication, Division, and Parentheses

### Lesson Practice

1. 33
2. 6
3. −15
4. 11
5. $48.00

### Test Preparation Practice

1. B
2. B
3. A
4. C
5. B

# Chapter 3
# Using Numerical Operations on Fractions

## Prime Factorization

Recall from chapter 2 that when two numbers are multiplied together, each number is called a factor, and the answer is called the product. This means that every product can be broken down into at least two factors. The process of separating a number into its factors is called factorization.

For example, what are two factors of 6?

3 and 2, or 1 and 6 because 3 times 2 is 6 and 1 times 6 is 6.

A number that has exactly two factors, 1 and itself, is called a prime number. A number with more than two factors (such as 6) is called a composite number.

**Example 1**   Identify the following numbers as prime, composite, or neither.

a)   14

b)   7

c)   1

## Solutions:

a)   14 is a composite number because the factors of 14 are 1 and 14 and 2 and 7. Since 14 has more than two factors, it is composite.

b)   7 is a prime number because it has only two factors, 1 and 7.

c)   1 is neither because 1 only has one factor, itself. Thus, it is neither prime nor composite. (NOTE: Similarly, 0 is neither because it has infinitely many factors.)

Every number can be written as a product of prime numbers. The process of writing a number as a product of prime numbers is called prime factorization.

Often, we use a factor tree to find the prime factorization of a number.

**Example 2**    **Find the prime factorization of 24.**

## Solution:

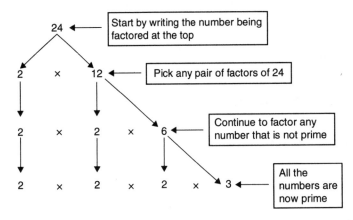

Once all the numbers are the bottom of the tree are prime, we stop factoring.

The prime factorization of 24 is $2 \times 2 \times 2 \times 3$.

**Example 3**    **Find the prime factorization of 48.**

## Solution:

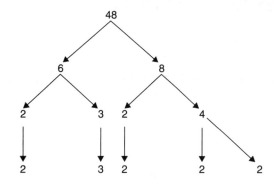

The prime factorization of 48 is $2 \times 2 \times 2 \times 2 \times 3$.

## Lesson Practice

For questions 1–4, identify the number as prime, composite, or neither.

1.  15 _composite_ ✓
2.  29 _prime_ ✓
3.  1 _neither_ ✓
4.  0 _neither_ ✓

For questions 5–8, find the prime factorization of the number.

5.  16 _2×2×2×2_ ✓
6.  28 _2×2×7_
7.  81 _3×3×3×3_ ✓
8.  102 _2×3×17_

## Test Preparation Practice

Circle the letter of the best answer.

1. How many prime numbers are in the list 1, 2, 3, 4, 5, 6, 7, 8, 9, 10?

   A. 3

   B. 4

   C. 5

   D. 6

2. Which number is not prime?

   A. 13

   B. 17

   C. 41

   D. 57

3. Jason said that he was thinking of a prime number between 20 and 30. Which of the following could be the number of which he was thinking?

   A. 21

   B. 23

   C. 25

   D. 27

4. What is the prime factorization of 18?

   A. $2 \times 3 \times 5$

   B. $2 \times 2 \times 3$

   C. $2 \times 3 \times 3$

   D. $1 \times 2 \times 3 \times 3$

## Least Common Multiple

To produce multiples of a number, take that number and multiply by some other whole number greater than zero.

For example, if we multiply 2 by 3, our answer is 6. Thus, 6 is a multiple of 2. Similarly, 24 is a multiple of 6 because 6 times 4 is 24.

Common multiples are numbers that are multiples of two or more other numbers.

For example, 12 is a common multiple of 2 and 3, because $2 \times 6 = 12$ and $3 \times 4 = 12$.

The least common multiple (LCM) is the smallest number that is a common multiple of two or more numbers.

To find the LCM of two or more numbers:

Step 1: Find the prime factorization of each number.

Step 2: Identify the greatest number of times each factor appears in the prime factorization.

Step 3: Multiply the prime factors identified in Step 2.

**Example 1**    **Find the LCM of 4 and 6.**

## Solution:

Step 1: Find the prime factorization of each number.

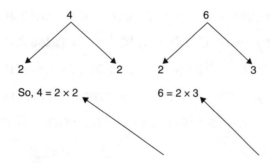

So, $4 = 2 \times 2$        $6 = 2 \times 3$

Step 2: Since 2 appears twice here and only once here, we identify that the greatest number of times 2 appears is twice. 3 only appears once.

Step 3: The LCM equals $2 \times 2 \times 3 = 12$.

**Example 2**    Find the LCM of 8 and 12.

Step 1:    Prime Factorization.

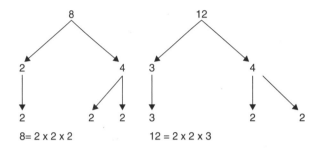

8 = 2 x 2 x 2            12 = 2 x 2 x 3

Step 2:    Identify the factors. Since 2 appears in three times in the factorization of 8 and only twice in the factorization of 12, we identify that the greatest number of times that two appears as a factor is three. 3 only appears as a factor once.

Step 3:    Multiply. LCM = 2 × 2 × 2 × 3 = 24.

Sometimes, it is simpler or more practical to find the LCM by simply listing several multiples of each number.

For example, what is the LCM of 4 and 5?

Some multiples of 4 are 8, 12, 16, and 20. Some multiples of 5 are 10, 15, and 20. Thus, the LCM is 20. This method is particularly useful when solving some real-life situation problems.

**Example 3**    At Fun City, U.S.A., guests can either ride the train or ferry from the hotel to the amusement park. Starting at 8:00 a.m. the train runs every fifteen minutes, while the ferry runs every 40 minutes. When is the next time that both will be leaving at the same time?

## Solution:

Since the train runs every fifteen minutes, starting at 8:00 a.m. its schedule will be 8:15, 8:30, 8:45, 9:00, 9:15, 9:30, 9:45, 10:00 and so on. The ferry's schedule will be 8:00, 8:40, 9:20, 10:00 and so on. Thus, the next time that both the train and ferry are leaving at the same time is 10:00 a.m.

## Lesson Practice

For questions 1 and 2, list the first 5 multiples of each number.

1. 20 _20, 40, 60, 80, 100_ ✓

2. 100 _100, 200, 300, 400, 500_ ✓

For questions 3 and 4, list the first 7 multiples of the two numbers, and then identify the LCM.

3. 8 and 14 _8 - 8, 16, 24, 32, 40, 48, 56   14 - 14, 28, 42, 56, 70, 84, 98   LCM = 56_ ✓

4. 6 and 9 _6 - 6, 12, 18, 24, 30, 36, 42   9 - 9, 18, 27, 36, 45, 54, 63   LCM = 18_ ✓

5. Find the LCM of 10 and 15 (Use prime factorization). _30_ ✓

6. If two runners are at the starting line of a track at 1:00 p.m. and one runner runs one lap every 12 minutes and the other runner runs a lap every 5 minutes, what time will it be when both runners are at the starting line of the track at the same time? _2:00 pm_ ✓

## Test Preparation Practice

Circle the letter of the correct answer.

1. What is the LCM of 9 and 15?

   A. 3

   B. 35

   C. 45

   D. 135

2.  Which number is a common multiple of 12 and 18?

    A.  24

    B.  36

    C.  48

    D.  60

3.  On a carnival ride, a red sign lights up every 5 seconds. The green sign lights up every 8 seconds. If both signs light up at the same time, how long will it be until they light up at the same time again?

    A.  5 s

    B.  8 s

    C.  20 s

    D.  40 s

4.  If soda cans are sold 6 in a pack and soda bottles are sold 10 in a pack, how many packs of soda cans and how many packs of soda bottles do you need to buy so that there is exactly the same number of cans as bottles?

    A.  3 packs of cans and 4 packs of bottles

    B.  4 packs of cans and 3 packs of bottles

    C.  3 packs of cans and 5 packs of bottles

    D.  5 packs of cans and 3 packs of bottles

## Fractions and Mixed Numbers

A fraction is a number that describes a ratio of two numbers. A fraction has two parts. The top number is called the numerator. The bottom number is called the denominator. For example, $\frac{4}{7}$ is a fraction where 4 is the numerator and 7 is the denominator. Fractions usually describe parts of a whole.

**Example 1**    **Write a fraction that represents the shaded portion of the figure.**

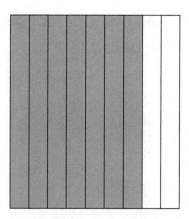

## Solution:

Since there are 7 shaded regions and 9 regions total, the fraction describing shaded region is $\frac{7}{9}$.

**Example 2**    **Write a fraction that describes the number of red cars in a parking lot if there are 35 red cars and 50 blue cars in a parking lot.**

## Solution:

To write a fraction, we need to know how many red cars are in the lot and how many cars total are in the lot. There are 35 red cars and there are 35 + 50 = 85 total cars in the lot. Thus, the fraction of red cars in the parking lot is $\frac{35}{85}$.

Fractions are also another way to describe a division problem. For example, 3 ÷ 5 is the same as writing $\frac{3}{5}$.

**Example 3** Write seven divided by eleven in fractional form.

## Solution:

$\frac{7}{11}$

When you combine whole numbers and fractions, you produce a mixed number. $2\frac{2}{3}$, $3\frac{1}{4}$, and $1\frac{1}{9}$ are all examples of mixed numbers. Mixed numbers can also be used to describe graphs.

**Example 4** Write a mixed number that describes the shaded area in the region below.

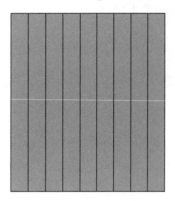 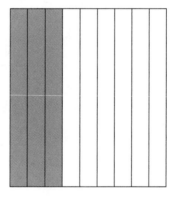

## Solution:

The first region is one whole and the second region has 3 shaded parts out of 9. Thus, the correct answer to this problem is $1\frac{3}{9}$.

A proper fraction is a fraction whose numerator (top number) is less than the denominator (bottom number). An improper fraction is a fraction whose numerator is greater than or equal to its denominator. Improper fractions and mixed numbers can both be used to represent the same number. Often it is convenient to use improper fractions.

**Example 5** Write an improper fraction to describe the shaded region shown in Example 4.

## Solution:

There are 12 shaded regions and 9 parts to a region. Thus, the improper fraction would be $\frac{12}{9}$. So, $\frac{12}{9} = 1\frac{3}{9}$.

How do we change mixed numbers to improper fractions and vice versa?

To change an improper fraction into a mixed number, simply do the division problem.

**Example 6**    Convert $\frac{14}{4}$ into a mixed number.

## Solution:

$$\frac{14}{4} = 4\overline{)14} = \begin{array}{r} 3r2 \\ 4\overline{)14} \\ -12 \\ \hline 2 \end{array}$$

Notice that instead of using "r" for remainder, we write the remainder as the numerator of the fraction and the divisor (in this case, 4) as the denominator.

$\frac{14}{4} = 3\frac{2}{4}$.

**Example 7**    Convert $\frac{11}{5}$ into a mixed number.

## Solution:

$$\frac{11}{5} = 5\overline{)11} = \begin{array}{r} 2r1 \\ 5\overline{)11} \\ -10 \\ \hline 1 \end{array} = 2\frac{1}{5}.$$

To convert a mixed number into an improper fraction, we use a two-step process. First, multiply the whole number and the denominator, then add the numerator to the answer to Step (1). The denominator for the mixed number will still be the denominator for the improper fraction.

**Example 8**    Convert $3\frac{3}{4}$ to an improper fraction.

## Solution:

First, determine the numerator. Step 1 is to multiply the denominator, 4, and the whole number, 3. $4 \times 3 = 12$. Secondly, add the numerator to the answer to Step (1), $3 + 12 = 15$. So, the numerator of the improper fraction is 15. The denominator stays the same. Thus, $3\frac{3}{4} = \frac{15}{4}$.

## Lesson Practice

For questions 1–4, write a fraction that describes the shaded region.

1.  $\dfrac{2}{3}$ ✓

2. 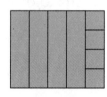 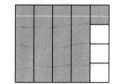 $1\dfrac{17}{20}$ ✓

3.  $\dfrac{1}{4}$ ✓

4.  $\dfrac{7}{8}$

For questions 5 and 6, write the division problem as a fraction.

5. $2 \div 9$ ___ $\dfrac{2}{9}$ ✓ ___

6. $11 \div 8$ ___ $\dfrac{11}{8}$ ✓ ___

For questions 7 and 8, convert the improper fraction into a mixed number.

7.  $\frac{17}{4}$   $4\frac{1}{4}$ ✓

8.  $\frac{15}{6}$   $2\frac{1}{2}$ ✓

For questions 9 and 10, convert the mixed number into an improper fraction.

9.  $3\frac{7}{8}$   $\frac{31}{8}$ ✓

10. $2\frac{4}{5}$   $\frac{14}{5}$ ✓

## Test Preparation Practice

Circle the letter of the correct answer.

1.  Which number is equal to $\frac{29}{7}$ ?

    A.  $3\frac{6}{7}$

    B.  $4\frac{6}{7}$

    C.  $5\frac{1}{7}$

    (D.)  $4\frac{1}{7}$

2.  If you ran for one hour and 15 minutes, which fraction represents the time in hours you ran?

    A.  $\frac{1}{15}$

    B.  $\frac{15}{60}$

    (C.)  $1\frac{15}{60}$

    D.  $1\frac{1}{15}$

3.  If a parking garage holds 200 cars and 65 are green, what fraction of the total cars is not green?

A.  $\dfrac{135}{200}$

B.  $\dfrac{65}{200}$

C.  $\dfrac{135}{100}$

D.  $\dfrac{65}{100}$

## Finding Equivalent Fractions and Reducing Fractions

Two fractions that have the same value are called equivalent fractions. To find an equivalent fraction, we either multiply both the numerator and the denominator by the same number, or divide the numerator and denominator by the same number.

In examples 1 and 2, replace [ ] with the number that makes the fractions equivalent.

**Example 1**   $\dfrac{3}{5} = \dfrac{[\ ]}{20}$

## Solution:

Since $5 \times 4 = 20$, we must multiply the numerator by 4 as well.

$\dfrac{3 \times 4}{5 \times 4} = \dfrac{12}{20}$. Thus $\dfrac{3}{5} = \dfrac{12}{20}$.

**Example 2**   $\dfrac{25}{60} = \dfrac{5}{[\ ]}$

## Solution:

Since $25 \div 5 = 5$, we must divide the denominator by 5 as well.

$\dfrac{25 \div 5}{60 \div 5} = \dfrac{5}{12}$. Thus $\dfrac{25}{60} = \dfrac{5}{12}$.

**Example 3** During baseball season, Dave reached base safely 44 out of 80 times. During softball season, Dave's sister only went to bat 20 times, but she reached base the same fraction of times that Dave did. How many times did Dave's sister reach base?

## Solution:

Since Dave reached base $\frac{44}{80}$ times and Dave's sister reached base $\frac{[\ ]}{20}$ times, we set these two fractions equal to one another. $\frac{44}{80} = \frac{[\ ]}{20}$. Since $80 \div 4 = 20$, we divide 44 by 4 as well. $44 \div 4 = 11$. So, Dave's sister reached base safely 11 times.

    To reduce fractions, also called writing the fraction in simplest terms, we divide both the numerator and denominator by the largest number that is a factor of each. This number is called the Greatest Common Factor (GCF). To find the GCF, list the factors of each number and choose the largest factor that appears in both lists.

**Example 4** Find the GCF of 6 and 15.

## Solution:

The factors of 6 are 1, 2, 3, and 6. The factors of 15 are 1, 3, 5, and 15. Thus, the GCF of 6 and 15 is 3.

**Example 5** Write $\frac{9}{12}$ in simplest terms.

## Solution:

Since the factors of 9 are 1, 3, and 9, and the factors of 12 are 1, 2, 3, 4, 6, and 12, the GCF of 9 and 12 is 3. Thus, we divide both the numerator and denominator by 3.

$$\frac{9 \div 3}{12 \div 3} = \frac{3}{4}$$

## Lesson Practice

For questions 1–2, determine which number both numerator and denominator were multiplied or divided by to change to the second number.

1. $\frac{3}{6}$; $\frac{9}{18}$ _____ 3 ✓

2. $\frac{10}{16}$; $\frac{5}{8}$ _____ 2 ✓

3. Write two equivalent fractions to $\frac{6}{12}$. $\frac{60}{120}$ $\frac{600}{1200}$ ✓

4. Write $\frac{15}{35}$ in simplest form. $\frac{3}{7}$ ✓

## Test Preparation Practice

Circle the letter of the correct answer.

1. Which fraction is NOT in simplest form?

   A. $\frac{3}{7}$

   B. $\frac{5}{9}$

   C. $\frac{2}{15}$

   D. $\frac{4}{8}$

2.  If Erin eats half of her candy bar and Justin eats the same fraction of his bag of chips, how many chips did he eat if there were 40 chips in the bag?

    A.  10

    B.  20

    C.  30

    D.  40

3.  On a ten-question test, Julia correctly answered 6 questions. On her next test, she answered the same fraction of questions correctly. How many questions did Julia get right if the test had 30 questions?

    A.  6

    B.  12

    C.  18

    D.  30

    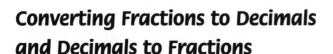

## Converting Fractions to Decimals and Decimals to Fractions

To change a fraction into a decimal, we divide the numerator by the denominator.

**Example 1**    Write $\frac{6}{8}$ as a decimal.

**Solution:**

$$\frac{6}{8} = 6 \div 8 = 0.75.$$

**Example 2**    Write $\frac{1}{3}$ as a decimal.

**Solution:**

$$\frac{1}{3} = 1 \div 3 = 0.33333... = 0.\overline{3}$$

**Example 3**   Write $3\frac{11}{17}$ as a decimal.

## Solution:

Since $3\frac{11}{17} = 3 + \frac{11}{17} = 3 + 11 \div 17 = 3 + 0.647 = 3.647$

To change decimals into fractions, we use the following steps:

1) identify the place value of the last decimal place,

2) then write the decimal as a whole number in the numerator of a fraction,

3) write the place value of the last decimal place as the denominator, and

4) reduce the fraction, if necessary.

**Example 4**   Convert 0.34 into a fraction.

## Solution:

Step 1:    Identify the place value of the last decimal place: 4 is in the hundredths place.

Step 2 and Step 3:    Write the decimal as a whole number in the numerator of a fraction and write the place value of the last decimal place as the denominator: $\frac{34}{100}$

Step 4:    Reduce the fraction: $\frac{34}{100} = \frac{34 \div 2}{100 \div 2} = \frac{17}{50}$.

**Example 5**   Write 2.75 as a mixed number.

## Solution:

$2.75 = 2\frac{75}{100} = 2\frac{75 \div 25}{100 \div 25} = 2\frac{3}{4}$.

## Lesson Practice

For questions 1–4, write the fraction as a decimal.

1. $\frac{5}{7}$ _0.714_ ✓

2. $\frac{10}{20}$ _0.5_ ✓

3. $\frac{9}{11}$ _0.81_ ✓

4. $\frac{65}{10}$ _6.5_ ✓

For questions 5–8, write the decimal as a fraction in simplest terms.

5. 0.25 _$\frac{1}{4}$_ ✓

6. 3.605 _$3\frac{121}{200}$_ ✓

7. 1.333333... _$1\frac{1}{3}$_

8. 1.002 _$1\frac{1}{500}$_ ✓

## Test Preparation Practice

Circle the letter of the correct answer.

1. Which decimal is equivalent to twenty-four hundredths?

   A. 2400.0

   B. 24.0

   C. 2.40

   D. 0.24

2.   Which of the following is equivalent to 0.65?

A. $\dfrac{65}{10}$

B. $\dfrac{65}{100}$

C. $\dfrac{11}{20}$

D. $\dfrac{12}{20}$

3.   Which of the following is the decimal equivalent of $\dfrac{28}{10}$?

A.  2.8

B.  28

C.  0.28

D.  280

# Adding and Subtracting Fractions and Mixed Numbers

To add or subtract fractions, the denominator of each fraction must be the same. The process of making each denominator the same is called "finding a common denominator." When adding or subtracting fractions with a common denominator, add or subtract the numerators and leave the common denominator alone. Simplify the fraction, if necessary.

**Example 1**   Add $\dfrac{3}{11} + \dfrac{6}{11}$

## Solution:

$$\frac{3}{11} + \frac{6}{11} = \frac{3+6}{11} = \frac{9}{11}$$

**Example 2**   Subtract $\dfrac{5}{12} - \dfrac{1}{12} = \dfrac{5-1}{12} = \dfrac{4}{12} = \dfrac{1}{3}$

To add or subtract fractions without common denominators, we must first find a common denominator and rewrite the fraction as an equivalent fraction with the common denominator. The common denominator is the LCM of the two denominators.

**Example 3**     Add $\dfrac{1}{4} + \dfrac{1}{2} =$

## Solution:

The LCM of 4 and 2 is 4. Thus, 4 is the common denominator. So, we rewrite both fractions with a denominator of 4.

$$\frac{1}{4} + \frac{1}{2} = \frac{1}{4} + \frac{2}{4} = \frac{1+2}{4} = \frac{3}{4}$$

**Example 4**     Subtract $\dfrac{5}{6} - \dfrac{3}{4} =$

## Solution:

The LCM of 6 and 4 is 12. So, 12 is the least common denominator of the two fractions. We rewrite both fractions with a denominator of 12.

$$\frac{5}{6} - \frac{3}{4} = \frac{10}{12} - \frac{9}{12} = \frac{1}{12}$$

To add mixed numbers, add the whole numbers and add the fractions. When subtracting the mixed numbers, you may need to borrow from the whole number first, and then subtract the whole numbers and subtract the fractions.

**Example 5**     Add $3\dfrac{4}{5} + 5\dfrac{1}{7} =$

## Solution:

Separate the mixed numbers, add the whole numbers together, and add the fractions together.

$$3\frac{4}{5} + 5\frac{1}{7} = 3 + 5 + \frac{4}{5} + \frac{1}{7} = 8 + \frac{28}{35} + \frac{5}{35} = 8 + \frac{33}{35} = 8\frac{33}{35}$$

**Example 6**    Subtract $6\frac{11}{16} - 4\frac{5}{8} =$

## Solution:

Separate the mixed numbers and subtract the whole numbers together and subtract the fractions together.

$$6\frac{11}{16} - 4\frac{5}{8} = (6-4) + \left(\frac{11}{16} - \frac{5}{8}\right) = 2 + \left(\frac{11}{16} - \frac{10}{16}\right) = 2 + \frac{1}{16} = 2\frac{1}{16}.$$

**Example 7**    If a wooden board is $7\frac{11}{16}$ feet long and must be cut down to $6\frac{1}{4}$ feet long, how much wood needs to be cut off?

## Solution:

We need to subtract the two distances.

$$7\frac{11}{16} - 6\frac{1}{4} = (7-6) + \left(\frac{11}{16} - \frac{1}{4}\right) = 1 + \left(\frac{11}{16} - \frac{4}{16}\right) = 1 + \frac{7}{16} = 1\frac{7}{16}$$

Thus, $1\frac{7}{16}$ feet need to be cut off.

**Example 8**    Subtract $7\frac{1}{10} - 4\frac{3}{5} =$

## Solution:

$7\frac{1}{10} - 4\frac{3}{5} = 7\frac{1}{10} - 4\frac{6}{10}$, since $\frac{6}{10}$ is greater than $\frac{1}{10}$, we must borrow $\frac{10}{10}$ from 7. Thus,

$$7\frac{1}{10} - 4\frac{3}{5} = 7\frac{1}{10} - 4\frac{6}{10} = 6\frac{11}{10} - 4\frac{6}{10} = (6-4) + \left(\frac{11}{10} - \frac{6}{10}\right) = 2\frac{5}{10} = 2\frac{1}{2}.$$

## Lesson Practice

For questions 1–4, add or subtract the fractions and then write the answer in simplest terms.

1. $\dfrac{3}{5} + \dfrac{1}{5} =$ _____ $\dfrac{4}{5}$ ✓

2. $\dfrac{11}{20} - \dfrac{3}{10} =$ _____ $\dfrac{1}{4}$ ✓

3. $\dfrac{7}{8} + \dfrac{2}{3} =$ _____ $1\dfrac{16}{21}$  ✗  $1\dfrac{13}{24}$

4. $\dfrac{9}{12} - \dfrac{1}{2} =$ _____ $\dfrac{1}{4}$ ✓

For questions 5–8, add or subtract the mixed numbers then write the answer in simplest terms.

5. $2\dfrac{9}{10} - 1\dfrac{1}{5} =$ _____ $1\dfrac{7}{10}$ ✓

6. $7\dfrac{1}{2} + 2\dfrac{3}{11} =$ _____ $9\dfrac{17}{22}$ ✓

7. $5\dfrac{2}{3} - 3\dfrac{6}{7} =$ _____ $1\dfrac{17}{21}$ ✓

8. $12\dfrac{10}{13} - 10\dfrac{2}{13} =$ _____ $2\dfrac{8}{13}$ ✓

9. How much longer is $\dfrac{7}{11}$ meters than $\dfrac{2}{7}$ meters? _____ $\dfrac{27}{77}$ meters ✓

10. What is the sum of $\dfrac{1}{3} + \dfrac{1}{2} + \dfrac{1}{12}$? _____ $\dfrac{11}{12}$ ✓

11. If Jim has $\dfrac{1}{3}$ of a candy bar and Debbie has $\dfrac{1}{5}$ of a candy bar, how much more candy bar does Jim have than Debbie? _____ $\dfrac{2}{15}$ ✓

## Test Preparation Practice

Circle the letter of the correct answer.

1. What is $\dfrac{2}{5} + \dfrac{3}{6}$?

   A. $\dfrac{27}{30}$

   B. $\dfrac{5}{11}$

   C. $\dfrac{30}{30}$

   D. $\dfrac{25}{30}$

2. Which of the following is $\dfrac{12}{25} - \dfrac{4}{5}$?

   A. $\dfrac{8}{25}$

   B. $-\dfrac{8}{25}$

   C. $-\dfrac{8}{20}$

   D. $-\dfrac{2}{5}$

3. If two-thirds of the pizza was left over from dinner and Stan ate one-sixth of the pizza the next day for lunch, how much of the pizza is now left over?

   A. $\dfrac{1}{3}$

   B. $\dfrac{2}{3}$

   C. $\dfrac{1}{2}$

   D. $\dfrac{5}{6}$

4.  If Timmy is $3\frac{2}{9}$ feet tall and the roller coaster requires a person to be $4\frac{1}{9}$ feet tall, how much taller does Timmy need to be so that he can ride the roller coaster?

   A.  $\frac{8}{9}$ feet

   B.  $-1\frac{1}{9}$ feet

   C.  $7\frac{3}{9}$ feet

   D.  $1\frac{3}{9}$ feet

## Multiplying and Dividing Fractions and Mixed Numbers

To multiply fractions, multiply the numerators and multiply the denominators. Simplify the fractions, if necessary.

**Example 1**   Multiply $\frac{1}{2} \times \frac{2}{3} =$

### Solution:

$$\frac{1}{2} \times \frac{2}{3} = \frac{1 \times 2}{2 \times 3} = \frac{2}{6} = \frac{1}{3}$$

To multiply mixed numbers, first change the mixed number into an improper fraction and then multiply the numerators and denominators. Simplify if necessary.

**Example 2**   Multiply $2\frac{1}{4} \times 3\frac{2}{5} = \frac{9}{4} \times \frac{17}{5} = \frac{153}{20} = 7\frac{13}{20}$

**Example 3**   Multiply $1\frac{1}{3} \times 3\frac{1}{2} = \frac{4}{3} \times \frac{7}{2} = \frac{28}{6} = 4\frac{4}{6} = 4\frac{2}{3}$

To divide fractions, leave the first fraction alone, flip the second fraction and change the operation from division to multiplication. Simplify the fraction, if necessary.

**Example 4** Divide $\dfrac{3}{5} \div \dfrac{2}{3} = \dfrac{3}{5} \times \dfrac{3}{2} = \dfrac{9}{10}$

To divide mixed numbers, first change the mixed number into an improper fraction and then flip the second fraction and change the operation from division to multiplication. Simplify the fraction, if necessary.

**Example 5** Divide $2\dfrac{2}{3} \div 1\dfrac{4}{5} = \dfrac{8}{3} \div \dfrac{9}{5} = \dfrac{8}{3} \times \dfrac{5}{9} = \dfrac{40}{27} = 1\dfrac{13}{27}$

**Example 6** Divide $4\dfrac{1}{6} \div 2\dfrac{2}{5} = \dfrac{25}{6} \div \dfrac{12}{5} = \dfrac{25}{6} \times \dfrac{5}{12} = \dfrac{125}{72} = 1\dfrac{53}{72}$

**Example 7** If a cookie recipe calls for one-and-a-half cups of flour, and we need to make twice as many cookies as the recipe calls for, how many cups of flour should we use?

## Solution:

Twice means to multiply by two, so $1\dfrac{1}{2} \times 2 = \dfrac{3}{2} \times \dfrac{2}{1} = \dfrac{6}{2} = 3$ cups of flour.

## Lesson Practice

For questions 1–4, multiply the fractions and mixed numbers.

1. $\dfrac{4}{5} \times \dfrac{3}{7} =$ _____ $\frac{12}{35}$ ✓

2. $\dfrac{6}{11} \times \dfrac{3}{4} =$ _____ $\frac{9}{22}$ ✓

3. $2\dfrac{5}{6} \times 4\dfrac{1}{2} =$ _____ $12\frac{3}{4}$ ✓

4. $4\dfrac{2}{3} \times 2\dfrac{7}{8} =$ _____ $13\frac{1}{3}$ ✗ $13\frac{5}{12}$

For questions 5–8, divide the fractions and mixed numbers.

5.  $\dfrac{2}{3} \div \dfrac{3}{5} =$ _____ $1\frac{1}{9}$ ✓

6.  $\dfrac{3}{4} \div \dfrac{2}{7} =$ _____ $2\frac{5}{8}$

7.  $4\dfrac{1}{2} \div 3\dfrac{5}{6} =$ _____ $1\frac{4}{23}$

8.  $5\dfrac{3}{5} \div 2\dfrac{1}{4} =$ _____ $2\frac{22}{45}$ ✓

9.  If a $2\dfrac{1}{2}$ acre field is to be divided into 4 equal parts, how many acres is each part? _____ $\frac{5}{8}$ ✓

10. If 4 candy bars cost $3\dfrac{1}{3}$ dollars, how much does each candy bar cost? _____ $\frac{5}{6}$ ✓ dollars

11. If each $\dfrac{1}{2}$ hour of a jet-ski rental costs $25 dollars, how many half-hour sessions will $100 buy? _____ 4 sessions ✓

## Test Preparation Practice

Circle the letter of the correct answer.

1.  Dave walks on a track that is $\dfrac{1}{4}$ of a mile long. How far does Dave walk if he walks 10 laps around the track?

    A.  1 mile

    B.  2 miles

    C.  $2\dfrac{1}{2}$ miles

    D.  10 miles

2.  What is $\frac{2}{3}$ of $\frac{4}{5}$?

    A.  $\frac{3}{4}$

    B.  $\frac{5}{6}$

    C.  $\frac{6}{15}$

    D.  $\frac{8}{15}$

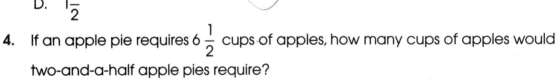

3.  If half of a pizza is to be divided up evenly among 3 people, how much pizza is each person going to receive?

    A.  $\frac{1}{6}$

    B.  $\frac{1}{6}$

    C.  $\frac{2}{3}$

    D.  $1\frac{1}{2}$

4.  If an apple pie requires $6\frac{1}{2}$ cups of apples, how many cups of apples would two-and-a-half apple pies require?

    A.  $16\frac{1}{4}$

    B.  $2\frac{3}{5}$

    C.  9

    D.  4

 # Chapter 3—Solutions

## Prime Factorization

### Lesson Practice

1. Composite
2. Prime
3. Neither
4. Neither
5. $2 \times 2 \times 2 \times 2$
6. $2 \times 2 \times 7$
7. $3 \times 3 \times 3 \times 3$
8. $2 \times 3 \times 17$

### Test Preparation Practice

1. B
2. D
3. B
4. C

## Least Common Multiple

### Lesson Practice

1. 20, 40, 60, 80, 100
2. 100, 200, 300, 400, 500
3. 8, 16, 24, 32, 40, 48, 56
   14, 28, 42, 56, 70, 84, 98
   LCM = 56
4. 6, 12, 18, 24, 30, 36, 42
   9, 18, 27, 36, 45, 54, 63
   LCM = 18

5. $10 = 2 \times 5, 15 = 3 \times 5,$
   LCM $= 2 \times 3 \times 5 = 30$
6. 2:00 pm

### Test Preparation Practice

1. C
2. B
3. D
4. D

## Fractions and Mixed Numbers

### Lesson Practice

1. $\dfrac{16}{24} = \dfrac{4}{6} = \dfrac{2}{3}$

2. $4\dfrac{5}{8}$   $1\dfrac{17}{20}$

3. $\dfrac{1}{4}$

4. $3\dfrac{1}{2}$

5. $\dfrac{2}{9}$

6. $1\dfrac{1}{8}$   $1\dfrac{3}{8}$

7. $4\dfrac{1}{4}$

8. $2\dfrac{3}{6} = 2\dfrac{1}{2}$

9. $\dfrac{31}{8}$

10. $\dfrac{14}{5}$

### Test Preparation Practice

1. D
2. C
3. A

## Finding Equivalent Fractions and Reducing Fractions

### Lesson Practice

1. 3
2. 2
3. $\dfrac{1}{2}$, $\dfrac{2}{4}$, answers may vary
4. $\dfrac{3}{7}$

### Test Preparation Practice

1. D
2. B
3. C

# Converting Fractions to Decimals and Decimals to Fractions

## Lesson Practice

1. 0.714

2. 0.5

3. 0.818181...

4. 6.5

5. $\dfrac{1}{4}$

6. $3\dfrac{121}{200}$

7. $1\dfrac{1}{3}$

8. $1\dfrac{1}{500}$

## Test Preparation Practice

1. D

2. B

3. A

# Adding and Subtracting Fractions and Mixed Numbers

## Lesson Practice

1. $\dfrac{4}{5}$

2. $\dfrac{5}{20} = \dfrac{1}{4}$

3. $1\dfrac{13}{24}$

4. $\dfrac{1}{4}$

5. $1\dfrac{7}{10}$

6. $9\dfrac{17}{22}$

7. $1\dfrac{17}{21}$

8. $2\dfrac{8}{13}$

9. $\dfrac{27}{77}$

10. $\dfrac{11}{12}$

11. $\dfrac{2}{15}$

## Test Preparation Practice

1. A

2. B

3. C

4. A

# Multiplying and Dividing Fractions and Mixed Numbers

**Lesson Practice**

1. $\dfrac{12}{35}$

2. $\dfrac{9}{22}$

3. $12\dfrac{3}{4}$

4. $13\dfrac{5}{12}$

5. $1\dfrac{1}{9}$

6. $2\dfrac{5}{8}$

7. $1\dfrac{4}{23}$

8. $2\dfrac{22}{45}$

9. $\dfrac{5}{8}$

10. $\dfrac{5}{6}$ dollars

11. 4

**Test Preparation Practice**

1. C

2. D

3. A

4. A

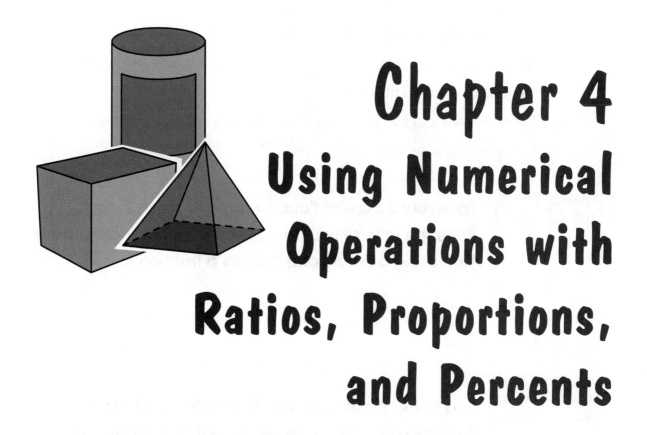

# Chapter 4
# Using Numerical Operations with Ratios, Proportions, and Percents

## The Ratio of Two Whole Numbers

Ratios are a comparison of two quantities. A ratio can compare a part to a part, a whole to a part, or a part to a whole. Ratios are usually written one of three ways.

1) Ratios can be written as words using the word "to." For example:

   a. The fruit juice solution is 3 parts water to every one part fruit juice. Thus, the ratio of the description is 3 to 1.

   b. The antifreeze is made up of 10 parts water to every 3 parts antifreeze. Thus, the ratio of the description is 10 to 3.

2) Ratios can be written using a colon. For example:

   a. The fruit juice solution is 3 parts water to every one part fruit juice. Thus, the ratio of water to fruit juice is 3:1.

   b. The antifreeze is made up of 10 parts water to every 3 parts antifreeze. Thus, the ratio of water to antifreeze is 10:3.

3) Ratios can be written as fractions. For example:

   a. The fruit juice solution is 3 parts water to every one part fruit juice. Thus, the ratio of water to fruit juice is $\frac{3}{1}$.

   b. The antifreeze is made up of 10 parts water to every 3 parts antifreeze. Thus, the ratio of water to antifreeze is $\frac{10}{3}$.

**Example 1**   **For every 3 cups of flour, a recipe requires 2 eggs. Write the ratio of flour to eggs as a ratio using the word "to," using a colon, and then as a fraction.**

## Solution:

3 to 2, 3:2, $\frac{3}{2}$.

**Example 2**   **In a deck of cards, there are 52 total cards and 13 of the cards are spades. Write the proportion of total cards to spades using the word "to," using a colon, and then as a fraction.**

## Solution:

52 to 13, 52:13, $\frac{52}{13}$.

**Example 3**   **In an elementary school, there are 123 first graders, 135 second graders, 112 third graders, and 106 fourth graders.**

   a) What is the ratio of first graders to third graders?

   b) What is the ratio of second graders to total students?

   c) What is the ratio of third and fourth graders to first and second graders?

## Solutions:

a) There are 123 first graders and 112 third graders, thus the ratio of first graders to third graders is 123 to 112.

b) There are 135 second graders but we must find the total numbers of students by adding the number of students in each grade. Thus, the total number of students is 123 + 135 + 112 + 106 = 476 students. Thus, the ratio of second graders to total students is 135 to 476.

c) We need to know how many students are in both third and fourth grade and how many students are in both first and second grade. There are 123 + 135 = 258 students in first and second grade and there are 112 + 106 = 218 students in third and fourth grade. Thus, the ratio of of third and fourth graders to first and second graders is 218 to 258.

## Lesson Practice

For questions 1–4, write the description as a ratio using a colon and as a fraction.

1.  there are 7 boys and 15 girls in gym class

    $7:15 / \frac{7}{15}$ ✓

2.  the acid solution requires 2 parts acid for every 1000 parts water

    $2:1000 / \frac{2}{1000}$ ✓

3.  the human body requires about 8 hours of sleep for every 16 hours awake

    $8:16 / \frac{8}{16}$ ✓

4.  a person ages 2 years for every 12 years that a cat ages

    $2:12 / \frac{2}{12}$ ✓    1  6

For questions 5–8, use the information in the chart below.

|  | **9th Grade** | **10th Grade** | **11th Grade** | **12th Grade** |
|---|---|---|---|---|
| **Boys** | 200 | 175 | 190 | 205 |
| **Girls** | 165 | 215 | 205 | 190 |

5.  What is the ratio of 10th graders to 11th grade boys? __390:190__ ✓

6.  What is the ratio of 9th graders to total students? __365:1545__ ✓

7.  What is the ratio of 11th grade boys to 11th grade girls? __190:205__ ✓

8.  What is the ratio of total students to 12th graders? __1545:395__ ✓

 **Test Preparation Practice**

Circle the letter of the correct answer.

1.  In the English alphabet, what is the ratio of vowels to consonants?

    A.  21:26

    B.  5:21

    C.  5:26

    D.  26:5

2.  A bag of marbles contains 10 red marbles, 15 blue marbles, and 5 green marbles. What is the ratio of red marbles to total marbles?

    A.  $\dfrac{10}{20}$

    B.  $\dfrac{20}{30}$

    C.  $\dfrac{10}{30}$

    D.  $\dfrac{30}{20}$

3.  If a fruit salad consists of apples, pears, and grapes, and the ratio of pears to apples is 3:4 and the ratio of grapes to apples is 5:4, what is the ratio of pears to grapes?

    A.  3 to 5

    B.  4 to 5

    C.  3 to 4

    D.  3 to 8

4.   In which word is the ratio of vowels to total letters 2:6?

   A.   BANANA

   B.   APPLE

   C.   TISSUE

   D.   GLAZED

## Making Comparisons with Ratios

Ratios can be used to make comparisons. When ratios are used for comparisons, they are usually referred to as rates and written as fractions. When the denominator of a ratio is 1, the comparison is called a unit rate. Often, a unit rate involves the word "per" such as miles *per* gallon or price *per* ounce.

**Example 1**   **If a 10-ounce can of diet soda costs 50 cents, what is the unit price in cents per ounce?**

## Solution:

Since there are 10 ounces of diet soda to every 50 cents, the ratio of ounces to cents is $\frac{50}{10}$, to write this ratio as a unit rate, we must divide both the numerator and denominator by 10. $\frac{50}{10} = \frac{50 \div 10}{10 \div 10} = \frac{5}{1}$. Thus, the unit rate is 5 cents per 1 ounce.

**Example 2**   **If Jim drives 400 miles in 8 hours, what is his unit rate in miles per hour?**

## Solution:

$\frac{400}{8} = \frac{400 \div 8}{8 \div 8} = \frac{50}{1}$. Thus, the unit rate is 50 miles per 1 hour.

**Example 3**    If there are 4 caramels for every 12 chocolates in a box, how many caramels are there in a box of 48 chocolates?

## Solution:

We need to solve the equation $\frac{4}{12} = \frac{[\ ]}{48}$. Since 12 × 4 = 48, we must multiply the numerator by 4 as well. Thus, 4 × 4 = 16. So, there are 16 caramels in a box of 48 chocolates.

**Example 4**    Shelley made 12 out of 25 free throws during the season. If she had shot 100 free throws, how many would we expect her to make?

## Solution:

Since her ratio of shots made to shots taken is $\frac{12}{25}$, we need to create an equivalent fraction with 100 as the denominator. Since 25 × 4 = 100, we need to multiply the numerator by 4 as well. Thus, we would expect Shelley to make 12 × 4 = 48 free throws.

**Example 5**    Which is a better purchase, a 10-oz. bag of chips for $0.70 dollars, or a 15-oz. bag of chips for $1.05?

## Solution:

We need to compare the unit-rate cost of each bag of chips. The unit-rate cost of the 10-oz. bag of chips is $\frac{0.70}{10} = \frac{0.70 \div 10}{10 \div 10} = \frac{0.07}{1}$ dollars per ounce. The unit-rate cost of the 15-ounce bag of chips $\frac{1.05}{15} = \frac{1.05 \div 15}{15} = \frac{0.07}{1}$ is dollars per ounce. Thus, both bags cost the same per ounce.

## Lesson Practice

In questions 1 and 2, find the missing number to make the ratios equivalent.

1.  $\dfrac{3}{5} = \dfrac{[\ ]}{20}$   _12_ ✓

2.  $4 : 7 = 12 :$ _____ _21_ ✓

For questions 3 and 4, find the unit rate of each ratio.

3.  $500 dollars for 25 hours of work = ___ _20_ ✓ dollars per hour

4.  $15.00 for 6 lbs. of beef = ___ _2.50_ ✓ dollars per pound

5.  If Jeremiah spends $20 dollars for 4 birthday gifts, how much would he spend if he bought 12 Christmas gifts? ___ _$60_ ✓

6.  If 15 gallons of gas cost $30 dollars, how much does 10 gallons of gas cost?

    ___ _$20_ ✓

## Test Preparation Practice

Circle the letter of the correct answer.

1.  What value of $x$ makes the following ratios equivalent? $\dfrac{2}{3} = \dfrac{x}{15}$

    A.  5

    B.  10

    C.  15

    D.  30

2. If a typical turkey requires 30 minutes per pound of turkey to cook, how many hours would a 4 lb. turkey be required to cook?

   A.  1

   B.  2

   C.  120

   D.  3

3. If there are 6 parts oil for every 5 parts vinegar in a salad dressing, how many parts of oil are there in a salad dressing that is 30 parts vinegar?

   A.  36

   B.  30

   C.  24

   D.  18

4. If an antifreeze solution consists of 1000 parts water for every 25 parts antifreeze, how much antifreeze is necessary for a solution that consists of 5000 parts water?

   A.  50

   B.  75

   C.  100

   D.  125

# Proportions

A proportion consists of two equal ratios. When proportions are written as equations, we solve the equations by cross-multiplying.

**Example 1**    Solve the following proportion for x. $\dfrac{12}{25} = \dfrac{24}{x}$.

## Solution:

To solve for $x$, cross multiply. $\dfrac{12}{25} = \dfrac{24}{x} \longrightarrow 12x = 24 \times 25$, thus, $12x = 600$, dividing both sides by 12, $x = 600 \div 12 = 50$.

| Example 2 | If 5 bags of popcorn at the movies cost $18 dollars, how much would 8 bags of popcorn cost? |
|---|---|

## Solution:

We set up a proportion of $\dfrac{18}{5} = \dfrac{x}{8}$. To solve the proportion for $x$, we cross multiply and get $18 \times 8 = 5x$. So, $144 = 5x$. Finally, dividing both sides by 5, $x = 144 \div 5 = \$28.80$. So, 8 bags of popcorn would cost $28.80.

| Example 3 | If a running back on a football team runs for 65 yards in 13 tries, how many yards should we expect him to run in 20 tries? |
|---|---|

## Solution:

We need to solve the proportion $\dfrac{65}{13} = \dfrac{x}{20}$. By cross multiplying, $65 \times 20 = 13x$, which means that $1300 = 13x$, dividing both sides of the equation by 13, $x = \dfrac{1300}{13} = 100$. Thus, we would expect the running back to run for 100 yards in 20 tries.

## Lesson Practice

For questions 1 and 2, solve the proportion for $x$.

1. $\dfrac{11}{20} = \dfrac{x}{80}$ _____ 44 ✓ _____

2. $\dfrac{5}{x} = \dfrac{25}{15}$ _____ 3 ✓ _____

For questions 3 and 4, use cross products to determine if the ratios form a proportion.

3. $\frac{3}{4} \overset{?}{=} \frac{15}{20}$ _____ Yes ✓

4. $\frac{4}{5} \overset{?}{=} \frac{18}{20}$ _____ No ✓

5. If the amount of cat food that a typical cat eats is proportional to the cat's weight, and a 4 lb. cat eats 1 cup of food per day, how much cat food will a 12 lb. cat eat per day? _____ 3 cups ✓

6. The ratio of boys to girls in a middle school is 3:2. How many girls would we expect in a class of 18 boys? _____ 12 girls ✓

7. For people over 6 feet tall, for every 2 inches of height, they tend to gain 15 lbs. To the nearest pound, how much more will someone weigh when they are 6 feet 5 inches tall than when they were 6 feet tall? _____ 38 lbs ✓

# Test Preparation Practice

Circle the letter of the correct answer.

1. What value of $x$ would make the following proportion true? $\frac{30}{x} = \frac{6}{10}$

    A. 300

    B. 3

    C. 5

    D. 50 ✓

2. If a speed boat can travel 500 miles on 25 gallons of gas, how far can the speed boat travel on 10 gallons of gas?

    A. 100

    B. 200 ✓

    C. 300

    D. 400

3. If a person is making cookies for a party and the recipe calls for 2 eggs to make 1 dozen cookies, how many eggs are required to make 600 cookies?

   A. 1200

   B. 600

   C. 300

   D. 100

4. If it takes 40 minutes to walk 2 miles, how long will it take to walk 5 miles?

   A. 1 hour and 40 minutes

   B. 2 hours

   C. 1 hour and 20 minutes

   D. 2 hours and 20 minutes

## Percents

Ratios that compare a number to 100 are called percents. Percents are written either as fractions with a denominator of 100, or as decimals.

| Example 1 | **Write 10% as a fraction.** |
|---|---|

## Solution:

To write a percent as a fraction, we write the percent as the numerator and 100 as the denominator and then simplify. Thus, $10\% = \dfrac{10}{100} = \dfrac{1}{10}$.

| Example 2 | **Write 10% as a decimal.** |
|---|---|

## Solution:

To convert a percent to a decimal, divide the percent by 100. Thus, $10\% = 10 \div 100 = 0.1$

**Example 3**   Write the ratio 15 out of 20 as a percent.

## Solution:

We set up the proportion $\dfrac{15}{20} = \dfrac{x}{100}$. Cross multiplying gives $1500 = 20x$, then dividing both sides of the equation by 20, $x = 1500 \div 20 = 75\%$.

**Example 4**   Fill in the following chart with appropriate equivalent decimal, fraction in simplest terms, or percent.

| Fraction | Decimal | Percent |
|----------|---------|---------|
| $\dfrac{3}{4}$ | | |
| | 0.34 | |
| | | 92 % |
| | | 134 % |
| | 0.333... | |

## Solution:

| Fraction | Decimal | Percent |
|----------|---------|---------|
| $\dfrac{3}{4}$ | $3 \div 4 = 0.75$ | 75% |
| $\dfrac{34}{100} = \dfrac{17}{50}$ | $34 \div 100 = 0.34$ | 34% |
| $\dfrac{92}{100} = \dfrac{23}{25}$ | $92 \div 100 = 0.92$ | 92% |
| $\dfrac{134}{100} = \dfrac{67}{50} = 1\dfrac{17}{50}$ | $134 \div 100 = 1.34$ | 134% |
| $0.3333... = \dfrac{1}{3}$ | $0.3333...$ | $0.3333... \times 100 = 33.333...\%$ |

## Lesson Practice

1. There are 50 states in the United States. If 32 states voted Democratic in an election, what percent of the states voted Democratic? ___64%___ ✓

2. Write the fractional equivalent of 14%. ___$\frac{7}{50}$___ ✓

3. Fill in the chart with the correct equivalent fraction, decimal, or percent.

| Fraction | Decimal | Percent |
|---|---|---|
| $\frac{9}{25}$ ✓ | 0.36 ✓ | 36% |
| $\frac{2}{5}$ | 0.4 | 40% |
| $\frac{9}{20}$ | 0.45 | 45% |
| $\frac{2}{3}$ | $0.\overline{6}$ | $66.\overline{6}\%$ |
| $\frac{6}{5}$ | 1.2 | 120% |

## Test Preparation Practice

Circle the letter of the correct answer.

1. Which of the following is equivalent to 12%?

   A.  1.2

   B.  .012

   C.  .12

   D.  12

2. Which of the following is a fractional equivalent to 95%?

     A. $\dfrac{9}{10}$

     B. .95

     C. $\dfrac{19}{20}$

     D. 9.5

3. If Jackie answered 14 out of 25 answers correctly on a quiz, what is her percentage score on the quiz?

     A. 14%

     B. 70%

     C. 175%

     D. 56%

4. If Kelly makes 35% of her 3-point shots in basketball, about how many shots would she be expected to make if she took 15 shots?

     A. 2

     B. 5

     C. 10

     D. 12

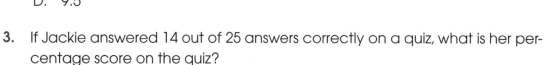

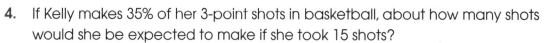

## Using Problem Solving and Proportions to Solve Word Problems

Many common real-life problems can be solved by using proportions. First, translate the word problem into a proportion, then solve the proportion by cross multiplying.

**Example 1**    **In a mayoral election in a small town, 70% of the people voted for the winning candidate. If the town has 2000 people, how many people voted for the winning candidate?**

## Solution:

Since $70\% = \dfrac{70}{100}$, we set up a proportion of $\dfrac{70}{100} = \dfrac{x}{2000}$, where $x$ is the number

of people who voted for the winning candidate. Then, we solve the proportion by cross multiplying.

$$\frac{70}{100} = \frac{x}{2000}$$
$$70 \times 2000 = 100x$$
$$140000 = 100x$$
$$140000 \div 100 = 100x \div 100$$
$$1400 = x$$

Thus, 1400 people voted for the winning candidate.

Alternatively, this problem can also be solved by noting that "of" means to multiply, thus 70% of 2000 = 0.70 × 2000 = 1400 people.

**Example 2**  **If 6 gallons of oil cost \$32.50, how much would 9 gallons of oil cost?**

## Solution:

We set up a proportion of gallons to cost, $\dfrac{6}{32.50} = \dfrac{9}{x}$, where $x$ is the cost of 9 gallons

of oil. Solve the proportion by cross multiplying.

$$\frac{6}{32.50} = \frac{9}{x}$$
$$6x = 292.5$$
$$6x \div 6 = 292.5 \div 6$$
$$x = 48.75$$

Thus, the cost of 9 gallons of oil is \$48.75.

**Example 3**  **If a basketball player misses 4 out of 25 free throws, what percentage of free throws does he make?**

## Solution:

Since the player misses 4 out of 25 free throws, then the player makes $25 - 4 = 21$ out of 25 free throws. To convert this ratio to a percentage, we first write it as a fraction, then as a decimal, then finally as a percent.

$$\frac{21}{25} = 21 \div 25 = 0.84 = 84\%$$

**Example 4**    **If a jacket that regularly costs $45.00 is on sale for $28.00, what percent is the discount?**

## Solution:

To find the percent of the discount, we must find the discount, then divide it by the original price and then convert the decimal into a percent.

Discount = Original Price − Sale Price = $45.00 − $28.00 = $17.00.

$$\frac{17}{45} = 0.37778 = 37.8\% .$$ Thus, the discount is about 38%.

### Lesson Practice

Solve each problem.

1. If Jamie read 60% of her assigned reading, and she was assigned 250 pages to read, how many pages did Jamie read? __150 pages__ ✓

2. A survey found that 87% of drivers come to a complete stop at stop signs. If 200 cars drive past that stop sign on a Wednesday, how many cars did not come to a full stop? __174 cars__ ✗ 26

3. If a car can go 250 miles on 10 gallons of gas, how far can it go on 15 gallons of gas? __375 miles__ ✓

4. If an electronics store has 200 televisions that must be sold by the end of the week and they sell 60% of them, how many televisions were not sold?
__80 televisions__ ✓

## Test Preparation Practice

Circle the letter of the correct answer.

1.  If a company advertises that its profits increased 32% last year, which of the following is a decimal representation of this increase?

    A.  0.32

    B.  3.2

    C.  32

    D.  .302

2.  If a car company says that its cars get 30 miles per gallon and its trucks get 60% of the miles per gallon that the cars get, how many miles per gallon do the trucks get?

    A.  15

    B.  18

    C.  21

    D.  24

3.  New cars lose about 60% of their value in the first four years after purchase. How much value has a new car that originally costs $30,000 lost after four years?

    A.  $12,000

    B.  $15,000

    C.  $18,000

    D.  $21,000

4.  What is the fractional representation of 75%?

    A.  $\dfrac{1}{4}$

    B.  $\dfrac{1}{2}$

    C.  $\dfrac{2}{3}$

    D.  $\dfrac{3}{4}$

# Chapter 4—Solutions

## The Ratio of Two Whole Numbers

### Lesson Practice

1. 7:15; $\frac{7}{15}$

2. 2:1000; $\frac{2}{1000}$

3. 8:16; $\frac{8}{16}$

4. 2:12; $\frac{2}{12}$

5. 390:190

6. 365:1545

7. 190:205

8. 1545:395

### Test Preparation Practice

1. B
2. C
3. A
4. D

## Making Comparisons with Ratios

### Lesson Practice

1. 12
2. 21
3. 20
4. 2.50
5. $60.00
6. $20.00

### Test Preparation Practice

1. B
2. B
3. A
4. D

## Proportions

### Lesson Practice

1. 44
2. 3
3. Yes
4. No
5. 3 cups
6. 12
7. 38 pounds

### Test Preparation Practice

1. D
2. B
3. D
4. A

## Percents

### Lesson Practice

1. 64%

2. $\frac{14}{100}$

3.

| Fraction | Decimal | Percent |
|----------|---------|---------|
| $\frac{36}{100}$ | 0.36 | 36% |
| $\frac{2}{5}$ | 0.4 | 40% |
| $\frac{45}{100}$ | 0.45 | 45% |
| 2/3 | 0.6666 ... | 66.666666% |
| $\frac{120}{100}$ | 1.2 | 120% |

### Test Preparation Practice

1. C
2. C
3. D
4. B

# Using Problem Solving and Proportions to Solve Word Problems

### Lesson Practice

1. 150
2. 26
3. 375
4. 80

### Test Preparation Practice

1. A
2. B
3. C
4. D

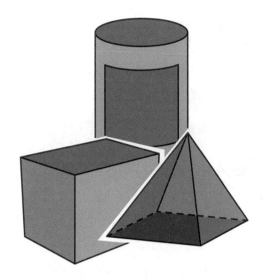

# Chapter 5
# Estimation

## Estimating with Whole Numbers and Decimals

In many real-life situations, an exact answer is not necessary and an approximation is an acceptable solution. We use estimation to find approximate answers quickly.

There are two primary methods of estimation. The first method is called rounding.

To round a whole number, we look at the digit to the right of the place value to which we wish to round. If the digit is 4 or less, we round down and the digit we are rounding stays the same. If the digit is 5 or greater, we round up and we add one to the digit we are rounding.

| Example 1 | Round the following whole numbers to the nearest tens place. |
|---|---|

a)   142

b)   255

c)   8

## Solution:

Since we are rounding to the nearest tens place, we must look at the digit in the ones place.

   a)   142: since 2 is in the ones place and is 4 or less, we round the 2 down to a
        0 and 142 rounds down to 140.

b)    255: since 5 is in the ones place and is 5 or greater, we round the 5 up to 10 and increase the tens place (in this case, 5) by one. Thus, 255 rounds up to 260.

c)    8: since 8 is in the ones place and is 5 or greater, we round the 5 up to 10 and increase the number in the tens place (in this case, 0) by one. Thus, 8 rounds up to 10.

**Example 2**    **Estimate the sum by rounding to the nearest thousand.**
**26,298 + 3,002 + 6,542 =**

## Solution:

We want to round each number to the nearest thousand, so we must look at the number in the hundreds place and round it correctly.

Thus, 26,298 rounds down to 26,000 because 2 is less than 5. 3,002 rounds down to 3,000 because 0 is less than 5, and 6,542 rounds up to 7,000 because 5 is greater. Thus, the sum of the numbers is about 26,000 + 3,000 + 7,000 = 36,000

A second method of estimation is called front-end estimation. In this case, we look only at the first numbers in the left most columns. It is important to note that the method of front-end estimation does not involve rounding.

**Example 3**    **Use front-end estimation to estimate the difference:**
**1,248 − 676**

## Solution:

Using front-end estimation, 1,248 is approximately 1,000 and 676 is approximately 600, thus 1,248 − 676 is approximately 1,200 − 600 = 600. So, the difference is about 600.

**Example 4**    **Use front-end estimation to estimate the sum:**
**34,098 + 11,675 + 970**

## Solution:

34,098 is about 30,000, 11,675 is about 10,000 and 970 is about 900, thus, using front-end estimation, 34,098 + 11,675 + 970 is about 30,000 + 10,000 + 970 = 40,970.

## Lesson Practice

In questions 1–4, use rounding to estimate the sum or difference.

1. Estimate 40.05 − 37.12 to the nearest tenth. _____3_____ ✓ (.0)

2. Estimate 175 + 4,509 + 20 to the nearest hundred. __4,700__ ✓

3. Estimate 46,098 − 25,768 + 15,576 to the nearest thousand.
   ___36,00___

4. Estimate 0.986 + 1.375 − 0.39 to the nearest tenth. ___2___ ✓ (.0)

In questions 5–8, use front-end estimation to estimate the sum or difference.

5. 109,805 − 4,500 __96,000__ ✗

6. 308 − 103 − 56 __150__ ✓

7. 1,200 + 3,409 − 1,575 __3,000__ ✓

8. 27 + 42 + 56 + 78 __180__ ✓

## Test Preparation Practice

Circle the letter of the correct answer.

1. If there are 432 students in 9th grade, 379 students in 10th grade, 446, students in 11th grade, and 346 students in 12th grade at a local high school, about how many students are there in all in the high school?

   A. 800

   B. 1100

   C. 1500

   D. 1800

2. Kelly went to the store with $20.00. She made three purchases. The first item cost $2.85, the second item cost $5.95, and the third item cost $10.40. About how much money did Kelly have left over after shopping?

   A. $1.00

   B. $8.00

   C. $10.00

   D. $16.00

3. A businessman travels all week for his job. The chart below tells how many miles he drove on each day of the week. Using front-end estimation, about how many miles did he drive total?

| Day of the Week | Miles Driven |
| --- | --- |
| Monday | 342 |
| Tuesday | 178 |
| Wednesday | 568 |
| Thursday | 95 |
| Friday | 245 |

   A. 800

   B. 1100

   C. 1400

   D. 1700

4. If Dave estimates the sum below by rounding to the nearest hundred, James estimates by rounding to the nearest ten, and Jennifer estimates by using front-end estimation, which of following statements is true?

$$672 + 145 + 309$$

   A. Dave's estimate is the greatest

   B. James's estimate is the greatest

   C. Jennifer's estimate is the greatest

   D. All three have the same estimate

# Estimating Products and Quotients

When estimating the answer to a multiplication problem, we try to use either rounding or front-end estimation to change the multiplication problem into numbers that can be easily multiplied mentally.

**Example 1**     Estimate 95 × 9

## Solution:

Since 95 is approximately 100 and 9 is approximately 10, we can say that 95 × 9 is about 100 × 10 = 1000.

**Example 2**     Jesse's book report is 45 sentences long. If Jesse's sentences are about 8 words each, about how many words long is Jesse's book report?

## Solution:

We round 45 up to 50 and 8 up to 10, thus, by multiplying 50 and 10, Jesse's book report is about 500 words long.

When estimating quotients, we estimate by using compatible numbers. That means that we estimate each of the numbers by using numbers that are easy to divide mentally.

**Example 3**     Estimate the quotient of 108 and 52.

## Solution:

We approximate 108 and 52 by using 100 and 50 because 100 ÷ 50 = 2.

**Example 4**     Estimate 608 ÷ 55

## Solution:

We estimate 608 ÷ 55 by using 600 ÷ 60 = 10.

### Lesson Practice

For questions 1–4, estimate the product.

1.  $2.98 \times 4.35$ _____ 12 ✓
2.  $678 \times 310$ _____ 2,100 ✓
3.  $29 \times 2598$ _____ 16,800 ✗
4.  $252 \times 0.098$ _____ 2.5 ✗

For questions 5–8, estimate the quotient by dividing compatible numbers.

5.  $252 \div 9$ _____ 25 ✓
6.  $87 \div 11$ _____ ✓
7.  $65 \div 6.8$ _____ 10 ✓
8.  $1220 \div 96$ _____ 12 ✓

9.  If a car weighs 4,512 pounds, about how much would 10 cars weigh? _____ 45,000

10. A computer company sold 25 computers to a business. The total bill came to $23,048.00. About how much did the computer company charge per computer? _____ 1,000 ✓

11. About how many gallons of gas will thirty dollars buy if gas costs $1.90 per gallon? _____ 60 ÷ 15

12. If one bucket of paint covers an area of approximately 200 ft², how many buckets of paint need to be purchased to paint a ceiling with an area of 1,372 ft²? _____ 70 ÷ 7

## Test Preparation Practice

Circle the letter of the best answer.

1. If a survey finds that 5,104 cars pass through an intersection during a 24-hour period, about how many cars pass through that intersection per hour?

   A. 100

   B. 200

   C. 300

   D. 400

2. A tourist wants to buy a souvenir in Guatemala. The souvenir costs 500 quetzals. At that time, one U.S. dollar is equal to 9.8 Guatemalan quetzals. About how many U.S. dollars does the souvenir cost?

   A. 30

   B. 40

   C. 50

   D. 60

3. Which of the following products is about 300?

   A. $14.02 \times 9.9$

   B. $7.8 \times 20.3$

   C. $36.8 \times 29.3$

   D. $29.6 \times 9.7$

4. Which of the following quotients is approximately 12?

   A. $72.2 \div 9.1$

   B. $37.3 \div 3.2$

   C. $562.5 \div 21.8$

   D. $476.1 \div 14.3$

# Chapter 5—Solutions

## Estimating with Whole Numbers and Decimals

### Lesson Practice

1. 3.0
2. 4,700
3. 36,000
4. 2.0
5. 104,000
6. 150
7. 3,000
8. 180

### Test Preparation Practice

1. C
2. A
3. C
4. B

## Estimating Products and Quotients

### Lesson Practice

1. 12
2. 2,100
3. 7,800
4. 25
5. 25
6. 8
7. 10
8. 12
9. 45,000 pounds

10. $1,000.00
11. 15
12. 7

### Test Preparation Practice

1. B
2. C
3. D
4. B

# Unit II

## Geometry and Measurement

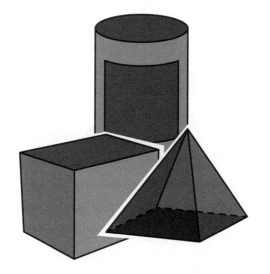

# Chapter 6
# Geometric Properties

## Properties of Lines, Rays, Angles, Line Segments, Parallel Lines, Perpendicular Lines, and Intersecting Lines

A line is all of the points in a straight path. Lines continue forever in both directions.

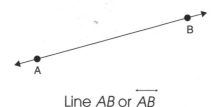

Line *AB* or $\overleftrightarrow{AB}$

A piece of a line with two endpoints is called a line segment.

Line Segment *FG* or $\overline{FG}$

A ray is a part of a line with one endpoint. Rays continue forever in one direction.

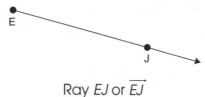

Ray *EJ* or $\overrightarrow{EJ}$

When two rays are connected with a common endpoint, they form an angle. The common endpoint is called the vertex of the angle.

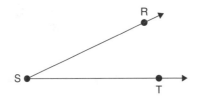

Angle *RST* or ∠*RST* or ∠*TSR* or ∠*S*

*S* is the vertex of angle *RST*.

| Example 1 | Given the following diagram, answer the questions that follow. |

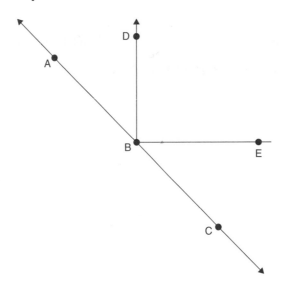

a) Name two angles that have *B* as a vertex. _____

b) Name one ray in the diagram. _____

c) Name one line segment in the diagram. _____

## Solutions:

a) ∠*ABD* and ∠*DBC*

b) $\overrightarrow{BA}$ or $\overrightarrow{BD}$ or $\overrightarrow{BC}$

c) $\overline{BE}$

When lines cross, they are called intersecting lines.

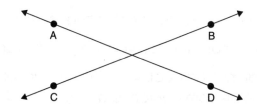

Lines *AD* and *BC* are intersecting lines

If lines do not cross, they are called parallel lines.

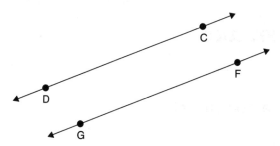

Lines *DC* and *GF* are parallel lines

If lines cross at right angles, they are called perpendicular lines.

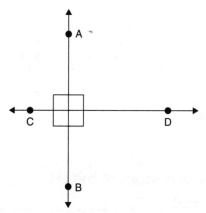

Lines *AB* and *CD* are perpendicular lines

**Example 2**    **Answer true or false for the following statements.**

a) Lines that intersect and form 90-degree angles are called perpendicular lines.

_____

b) Lines can be both perpendicular and parallel. _____

c) Parallel lines are always the same distance apart from one another.

_____

## Solutions:

a)    True. Perpendicular lines intersect at right angles, which measure 90 degrees.

b)    False. Parallel lines do not intersect while perpendicular lines do intersect.

c)    True. Parallel lines do not intersect, since the lines are always straight, the lines must always remain the same distance apart.

 **Lesson Practice**

For questions 1–6, use the diagram below.

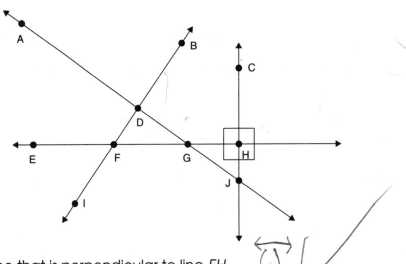

1.    Name a line that is perpendicular to line *EH*. _____

2.    What is the vertex of angle ∠*EFD*? _____

3.    True or false, line *AD* is parallel to line *CJ*. _____

4.    True or false, line *BF* is parallel to line *CJ*. _____

5.    Name a right angle in the diagram. _____

6.    True or false, line *AG* and line *EF* are intersecting lines. _____

## Test Preparation Practice

Circle the letter of the correct answer.

1.  Which of the following statements is true?

    A.  Perpendicular lines are intersecting lines.

    B.  Parallel lines are intersecting lines.

    C.  Parallel lines intersect at right angles.

    D.  Perpendicular lines do not intersect.

2.  Which of the following statements is NOT true?

    A.  A ray extends forever in one direction.

    B.  An angle is formed by two lines with a common endpoint.

    C.  A line segment is part of a line.

    D.  A line extends forever in both directions.

For questions 3 and 4, use the diagram below.

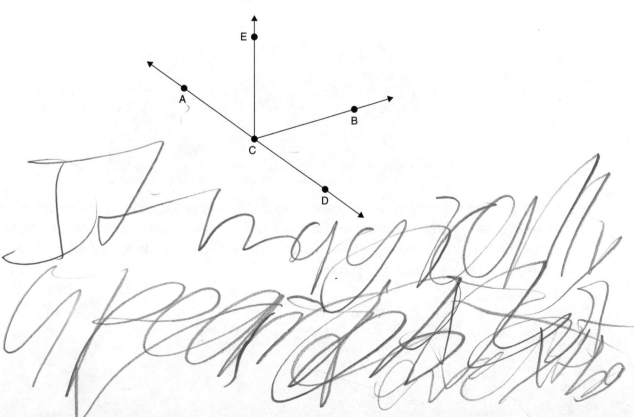

3. Which angle does NOT share a common side with angle *ACE*?

   A. *ECD*

   B. *ACB*

   C. *DCE*

   D. *BCD*

4. Which of the following is a line?

   A. *AD*

   B. *CE*

   C. *CD*

   D. *CB*

## Measuring Angles with a Protractor and Classifying Triangles by Angle Measure and Side Length

When we measure angles, we use a tool called a protractor. Angles are measured in degrees (°).

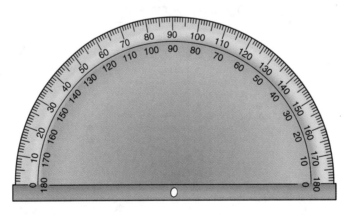

To use the protractor, place the center dot of the protractor on the vertex of the angle. To determine whether to read the inner or outer scale, we must look at which scale the ray passes through 0°. Then, we read the same scale to see where the other ray passes through the protractor.

| **Example 1** | Using the protractor, what is the measure of angle *DEF*? |

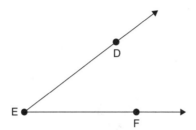

## Solution:

Place the center of the protractor on the vertex of the angle.

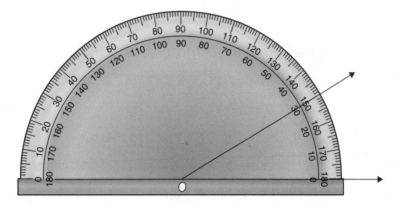

Since the lower ray passes through 0° on the inner scale, we use the inner scale to read the measure of the angle. The measure of the angle is 30°.

Angles can be classified by their measure. Angles that are less than 90° are called acute angles. Angles that measure exactly 90° are called right angles. Angles that measure between 90° and 180° are called obtuse angles. Angles that measure exactly 180° are called straight angles.

| Example 2 | Classify the following angles as acute, right, obtuse or straight. |
|---|---|

a)  $\angle A = 97°$ _____

b)  $\angle BCD = 176°$ _____

c)  $\angle DEF = 90°$ _____

d)  $\angle XYZ = 45°$ _____

e)  $E$ _____

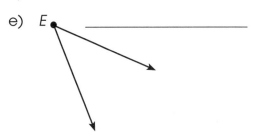

## Solution:

a)  $\angle A$ is obtuse because 97° is greater than 90° and less than 180°.

b)  $\angle BCD$ is obtuse because 176° is greater than 90° and less than 180°.

c)  $\angle DEF$ is a right angle because it measures 90°.

d)  $\angle XYZ$ is an acute angle because 45° is less than 90°.

e)  $\angle E$ is an acute angle because the angle is smaller than a right angle.

Just like angles can be classified by their measure, triangles can be classified by the size of their angles as well. Triangles have three angles. The three angles of a triangle always add up to 180°.

| Example 3 | Find the measure of angle *A* in the triangle below. |
|---|---|

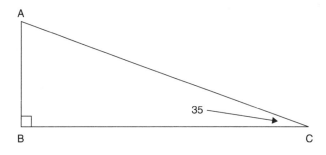

## Solution:

Since this is a right triangle, $\angle B = 90°$ and $\angle C = 35°$. Since the angles of any triangle add up to 180°, we know that the third angle, $\angle A = 180° - (90° + 35°) = 180° - 125° = 55°$.

When we classify triangles by angle measure, there are three possibilities.

| Acute Triangle | Right Triangle | Obtuse Triangle |
|---|---|---|
| All three angles are acute angles—each angle measures less than 90°. | Exactly one angle is a right angle—it measures 90°. | Exactly one angle is an obtuse angle—it measures greater than 90°, but less than 180°. |
| | | |

**Example 4**    **Classify the following triangles as acute, right or obtuse.**

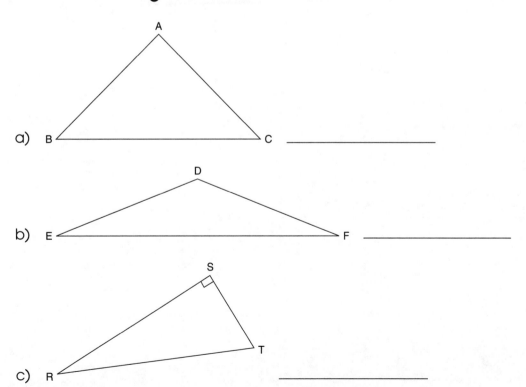

a) B _____

b) E _____

c) R _____

## Solutions:

a)   △ABC is an acute triangle because all three angles are acute.

b)   △DEF is an obtuse triangle because ∠D is an obtuse angle.

c)   △RST is a right triangle because ∠S is a right angle.

Triangles can also be classified by the lengths of their sides.

| Equilateral Triangle | Isosceles Triangle | Scalene Triangle |
|---|---|---|
| All three sides have the same length. | Two sides have the same length. | None of the sides have the same length. |
|  |  |  |

---

**Example 5**   **Classify the following triangles as equilateral, isosceles, or scalene.**

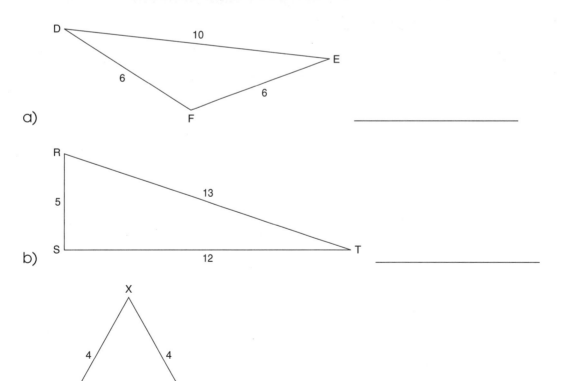

a)   _____

b)   _____

c)   _____

## Solutions:

a)   △DEF is an isosceles triangle because two sides have the same length.

b)   △RST is a scalene triangle because none of the sides have the same length.

c)   △XYZ is an equilateral triangle because all three sides have the same length.

### Lesson Practice

For questions 1–3, classify the triangle by both its angles (acute, right, or obtuse) and its sides (equilateral, isosceles, or scalene).

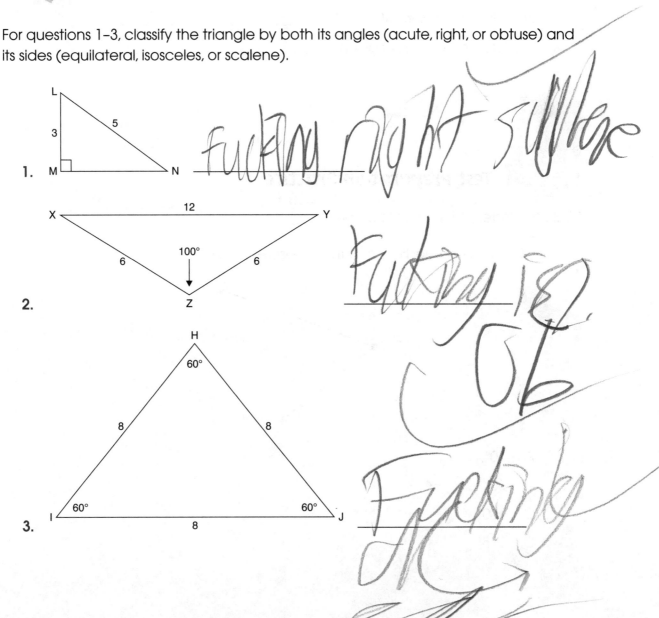

1.

2.

3.

For questions 4–5, use angle ABC as shown below on the protractor.

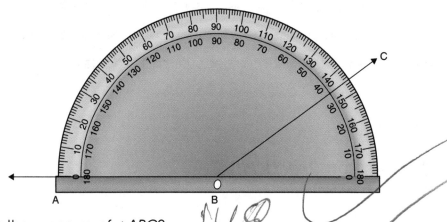

4.   What is the measure of ∠ABC?  _____

5.   Is ∠ABC acute, right, or obtuse?  _____

## Test Preparation Practice

Circle the letter of the correct answer.

1.   What is the best estimate of the measure of ∠DEF?

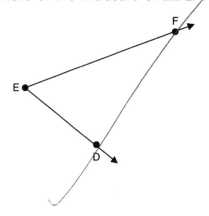

A.   10°

B.   60°

C.   100°

D.   175°

2.   If a triangle has two angles that add up to 100°, what is the measure of the third angle?

   A.   100°

   B.   90°

   C.   80°

   D.   10°

3.   Which of the following triangle combinations is impossible?

   A.   acute and equilateral

   B.   acute and scalene

   C.   right and isosceles

   D.   obtuse and equilateral

4.   If an isosceles triangle has one side of length 10 and one side of length 12, what could possibly be the length of the third side?

   A.   8

   B.   9

   C.   10

   D.   11

5.   Which set of angles below could be the measures of three angles of a triangle?

   A.   45°, 45°, 45°

   B.   90°, 90°, 45°

   C.   12°, 18°, 150°

   D.   100°, 80°, 5°

6.   What is the measure of ∠*XZY*?

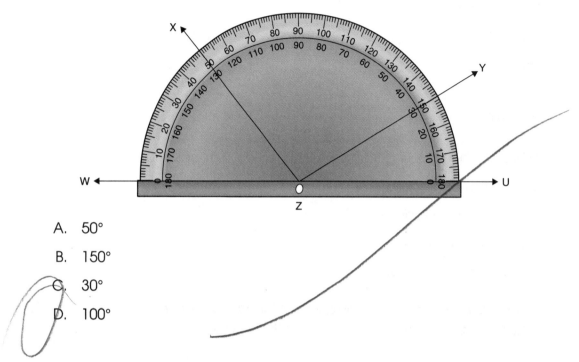

A.  50°

B.  150°

C.  30°

D.  100°

# Identify, Describe, Compare, and Classify Polygons and Circles

A circle is a closed figure whose points are all the same distance from one point in the center of the circle. We name circles by their center point. A line segment from the center point of the circle to any point on the circle is called a radius. A chord is any line segment from one point on a circle to another point on the circle. If a chord passes through the center of a circle, it is called a diameter. A diameter is twice as long as a radius.

**Example 1**    **The following questions refer to circle *O*.**

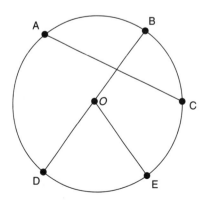

a)    What point is the center of the circle? _____

b)    Name a radius in the circle. _____

c)    Name a chord that is not a diameter. _____

d)    Name a diameter. _____

## Solutions:

a)    $O$

b)    $\overline{OE}$

c)    $\overline{AC}$

d)    $\overline{BD}$

A polygon is any closed figure whose sides are line segments. If all of the sides of the polygon are the same and all of the angles of the polygon are equal, then the polygon is called a regular polygon. Polygons are classified by their number of sides.

| Name of Polygon | Number of Sides |
|---|---|
| Triangle | 3 |
| Quadrilateral | 4 |
| Pentagon | 5 |
| Hexagon | 6 |
| Heptagon | 7 |
| Octagon | 8 |
| Decagon | 10 |
| $n$-gon | $n$ |

Quadrilaterals have their own classification and are identified by their sides and angles.

A parallelogram is a quadrilateral whose opposite sides are the same length and congruent.

A rectangle is a parallelogram whose angles are all 90°.

A square is a rectangle whose sides are all equal in length and whose angles are all 90°.

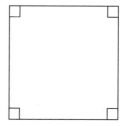

A rhombus is a parallelogram with four sides that are all the same length.

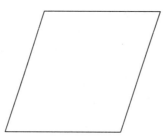

A trapezoid is a quadrilateral with exactly one pair of parallel sides.

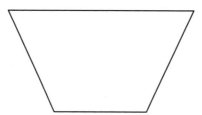

**Example 2**    Classify each of the figures below as accurately as possible.

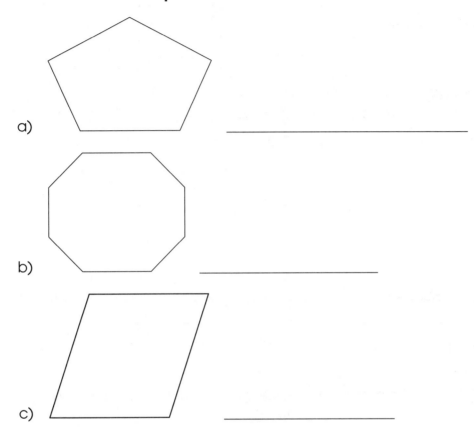

a) _____

b) _____

c) _____

## Solutions:

a)   Pentagon—the figure has five sides.

b)   Octagon—the figure has eight sides.

c)   Quadrilateral, Parallelogram, and Rhombus—the figure is four sided, has oppo-
     site sides that are parallel, and all four sides are of equal length.

## Lesson Practice

1. If a parallelogram has one side that is 10 inches long and another side that is 6 inches long, how long are the other two sides? _16 in. total_ ✓ _(10 in., 16 in.)_

2. List all of the possible classifications of the polygon below.

   _Rectangle, quadrilateral, Parallelogram_ ✓

3. Arrange the following polygons in order from the fewest number of sides to the largest number of sides: heptagon, decagon, triangle, and trapezoid.
   _Triangle, trapezoid, heptagon, decagon_ ✓

4. Which two quadrilaterals have four sides that are all the same length?
   _Rhombus, square_ ✓

5. In a circle, what is the name of the line segment that is drawn from the center of the circle to any point on the circle? _Radius_ ✓

## Test Preparation Practice

Circle the letter of the correct answer.

1. On circle O below, which line segment is a diameter?

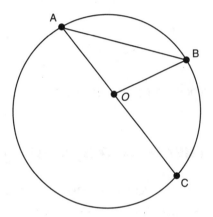

   A. $\overline{AO}$

   B. $\overline{AB}$

   C. $\overline{AC}$

   D. $\overline{OB}$

2. Which of the following shapes could NOT be regular?

   A. trapezoid

   B. rectangle

   C. square

   D. parallelogram

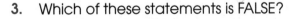

3. Which of these statements is FALSE?

   A. All rectangles are squares.

   B. All squares are rectangles.

   C. All parallelograms are quadrilaterals.

   D. All trapezoids are quadrilaterals.

4. Which of the following has the most sides?

   A. heptagon

   B. hexagon

   C. pentagon

   D. octagon

5. If a circle has a radius of 10 inches, how long is its diameter?

   A. 5 inches

   B. 10 inches

   C. 20 inches

   D. Not enough information to determine

## Similar Figures, Congruence, and Symmetry

Two figures are congruent if they have the same shape and size. Two figures are similar if they have the same shape, but not necessarily the same size.

**Example 1**  **Which of the following figures are congruent?**

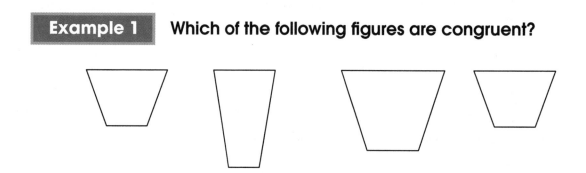

## Solution:

The first and last trapezoids are congruent because they have the same shape and size.

**Example 2**   **Which of the following figures are similar?**

 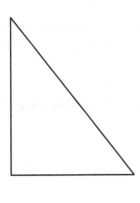  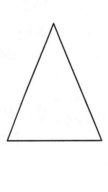

## Solution:

The first and second triangles are similar because they have the shape but are not the same size.

The parts of congruent figures that are the same are called corresponding parts.

**Example 3**   **Which line segment in △ *RST* corresponds to line segment *AB* in △*ABC*?**

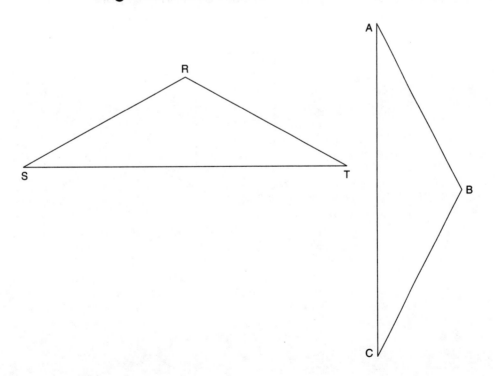

## Solution:

Line segment *RS* is congruent to line segment *AB*.

When two halves of a figure are the same, the figure has line symmetry. If a figure can be rotated and still look the same, it has rotational symmetry.

**Example 4**    **How many lines of symmetry does the following figure have?**

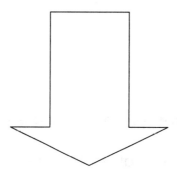

## Solution:

There is one line of symmetry that can be drawn on this figure.

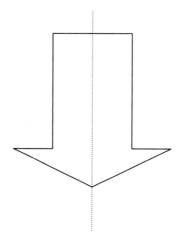

**Example 5**    Draw all the lines of symmetry on the following figure.

**Solution:**

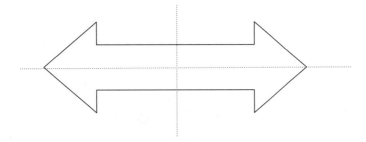

## Lesson Practice

1. Draw all the lines of symmetry in each of the figures below.

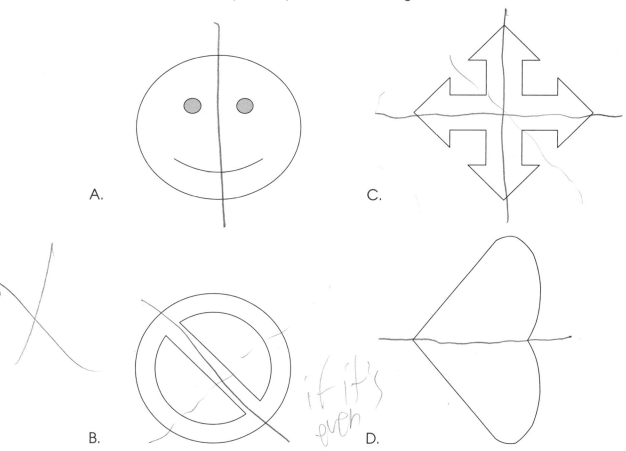

A.

C.

B.

D.

*if it's even*

2. Which of the figures above has/have rotational symmetry?

3.   Describe the following sets of figures as congruent, similar, or neither.

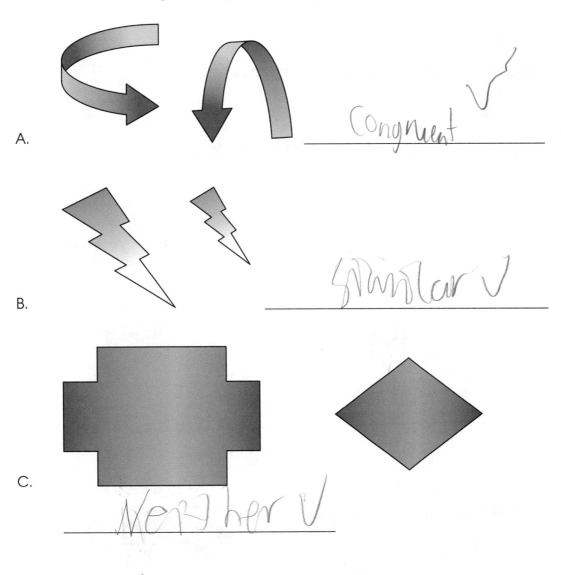

A.   _____Congruent ✓_____

B.   _____Similar ✓_____

C.   _____Neither ✓_____

## Test Preparation Practice

Circle the letter of the correct answer.

1. The following figures are congruent. How long is side *x*?

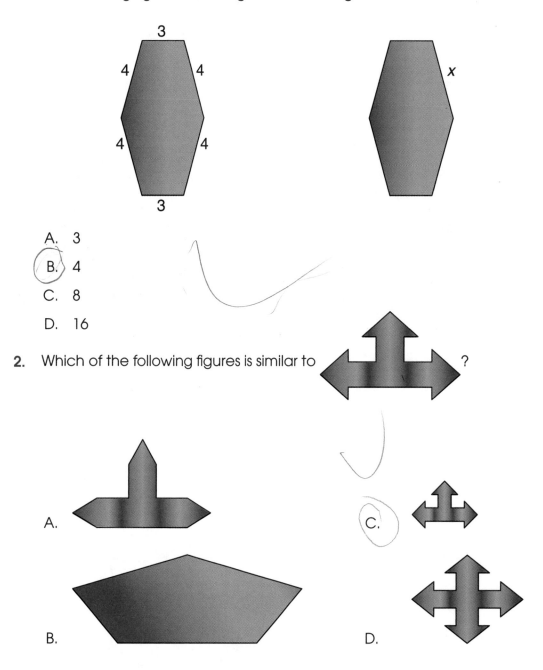

A. 3

B. 4

C. 8

D. 16

2. Which of the following figures is similar to

A.

B.

C.

D.

## Identify and Compare Properties of Cylinders, Prisms, Cones, Pyramids, and Spheres

Three-dimensional figures have faces, edges, and vertices. A face is any flat surface. An edge is the line segment formed where two faces meet and a vertex is the corner of a 3-dimensional solid (in other words, where more than two edges meet).

A 3-D polygon is called a polyhedron. All of its faces are polygons. Common examples of polyhedrons include pyramids and prisms.

A pyramid has one base that is a polygon and all of the other faces are triangles with a common vertex. The base can be any polygon. The pyramid is named by the shape of its base.

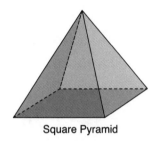

Square Pyramid

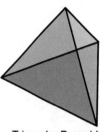

Triangular Pyramid

A prism has two congruent bases that are parallel. Prisms are named by the shape of the bases. The other sides of the prism are parallelograms.

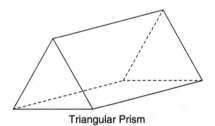

Triangular Prism

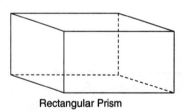

Rectangular Prism

A cylinder is shaped like a can. It has two congruent, circular faces. The faces are connected by a curved surface.

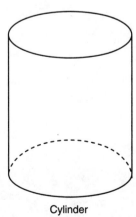

Cylinder

A sphere is a 3-dimensional circle. Every point on the surface of a sphere is equidistant from the center of a sphere.

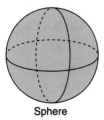

Sphere

A cone has a circular base and one vertex.

Cone

**Example 1**     **How many faces does each of the following figures have?**

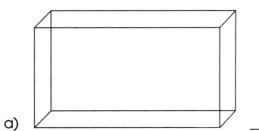

a) _____

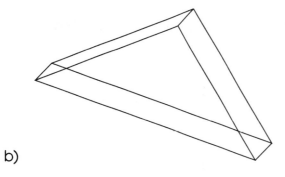

b)

## Solutions:

    a)   6

    b)   5

**Example 2**    **How many vertices does each of the following figures have?**

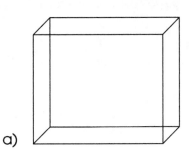

a)

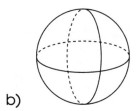

b)

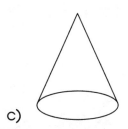

c)

## Solutions:

    a)   8

    b)   0

    c)   1

## Lesson Practice

For questions 1–4, identify the polyhedron represented by the figure.

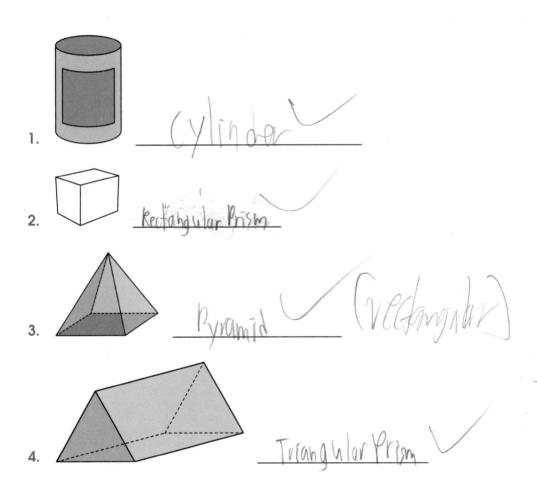

1. _____Cylinder_____ ✓

2. _____Rectangular Prism_____

3. _____Pyramid_____ ✓ (rectangular)

4. _____Triangular Prism_____ ✓

## Test Preparation Practice

Circle the letter of the correct answer.

1. How many faces does the following figure have?

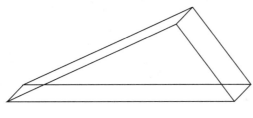

    A. 3

    B. 4

    C. 5

    D. 6

2. How many vertices does the cone below have?

    A. 1

    B. 3

    C. 5

    D. 7

3. What is the name of the figure pictured below?

A. cone

B. triangular pyramid

C. square prism

D. hexagonal pyramid

4. How many edges does a sphere have?

A. 0

B. 1

C. 2

D. 3

## Projections of Three-Dimensional Shapes

We can make projections of three-dimensional figures based on how they look when they are unfolded. When a three-dimensional figure is unfolded, we call the resulting two-dimensional figure a "net."

**Example 1**  **What would the net of the cube below look like?**

**Solution:**

If we wish to unfold a cube, we need to figure out how many sides the figure has. A cube has six sides, all of which are congruent squares.

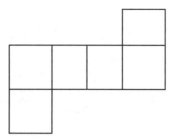

**Example 2**    **What three-dimensional figure has the following net?**

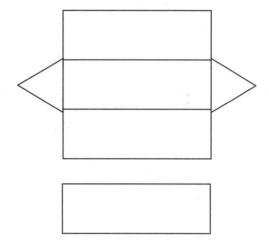

## Solution:

The bases of the figure are equilateral triangles. The remaining faces are rectangles. Thus, this figure is a triangular prism.

## Lesson Practice

For questions 1 and 2, sketch the net of the three-dimensional figure.

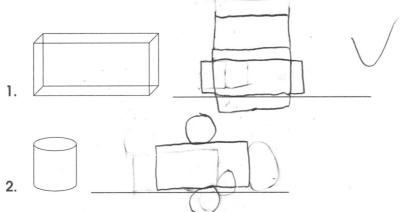

1.

2.

For questions 3 and 4, identify the three-dimensional figure associated with the net.

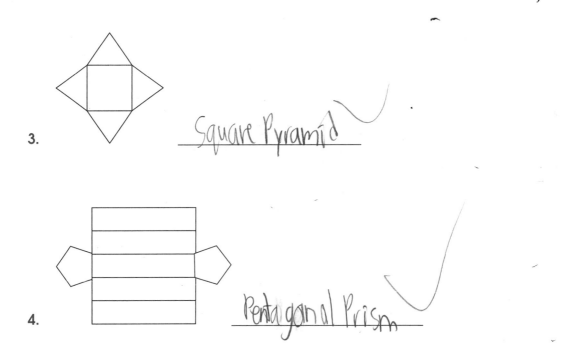

3. _Square Pyramid_

4. _Pentagonal Prism_

# Test Preparation Practice

Circle the letter of the correct answer.

1. If you look at a sphere from the side view, what shape would you see?

   A. square

   B. circle

   C. diamond

   D. rhombus

2. Which figure would look the same from the top, side, and bottom?

   A. rectangular prism

   B. cone

   C. square pyramid

   D. cube

3. Which of the following nets could be a cube?

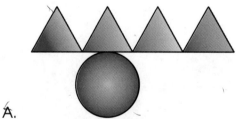

   A.

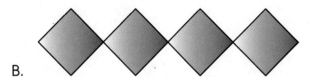

   B.

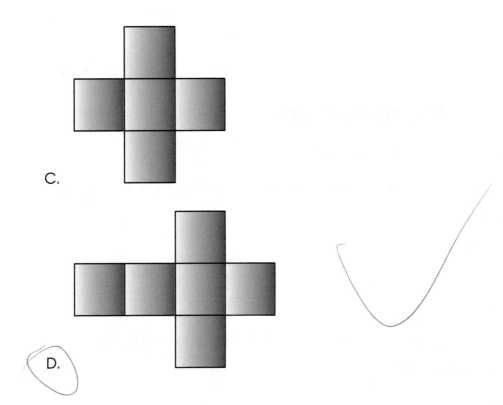

C.

D.

# Chapter 6—Solutions

## Properties of Lines, Rays, Angles, Line Segments, Parallel Lines, Perpendicular Lines, and Intersecting Lines

### Lesson Practice

1. *CH*
2. *F*
3. False
4. False
5. ∠*CHG*, answers may vary
6. True

### Test Preparation Practice

1. A
2. B
3. D
4. A

## Measuring Angles with a Protractor and Classifying Triangles by Angle Measure and Side Length

### Lesson Practice

1. right, scalene
2. obtuse, isosceles
3. acute, equilateral
4. 145°
5. obtuse

### Test Preparation Practice

1. B
2. C
3. D Equilateral triangles have three equal angles and triangles cannot have more than one obtuse angle
4. C
5. C
6. D

# Identify, Describe, Compare, and Classify Polygons and Circles

## Lesson Practice

1. 10 inches and 6 inches
2. quadrilateral, parallelogram, rectangle
3. triangle, trapezoid, heptagon, decagon
4. rhombus and square
5. radius

## Test Preparation Practice

1. C
2. A
3. A
4. D
5. C

# Similar Figures, Congruence, and Symmetry

## Lesson Practice

1.

   a.

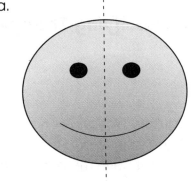

   b.

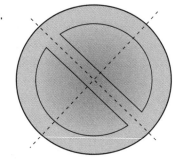

   c.

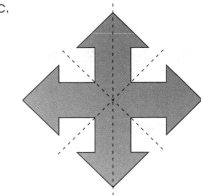

   d.

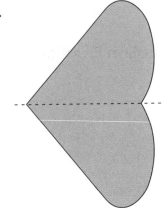

2. C.

3. a. congruent

   b. similar

   c. neither

1. B

2. C

# Identify and Compare Properties of Cylinders, Prisms, Cones, Pyramids, and Spheres

## Lesson Practice

1. cylinder

2. rectangular prism

3. rectangular pyramid

4. triangular prism

## Test Preparation Practice

1. C

2. A

3. D

4. A

## Projections of Three-Dimensional Shapes

### Lesson Practice

1.

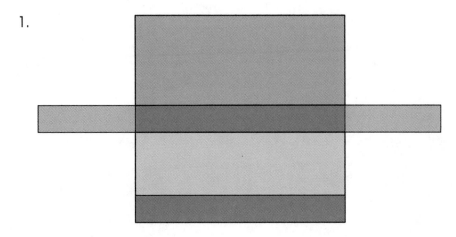

2.

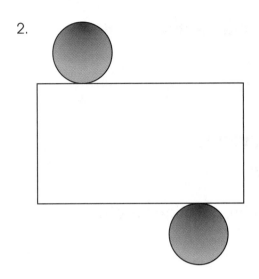

3. square pyramid
4. pentagonal prism

## Test Preparation Practice

1. B
2. D
3. D

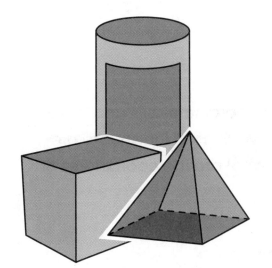

# Chapter 7
# Transforming Shapes and Coordinate Geometry

## Creating Geometric Shapes with Given Parameters

We can draw two-dimensional figures on a coordinate plane. Coordinate planes are a grid of horizontal and vertical lines. Coordinates are ordered pairs of numbers that tell where a point is located on the coordinate plane. The horizontal axis is called the *x*-axis and the vertical axis is called the *y*-axis. The ordered pair that gives the location of a point is always written (*x*, *y*). The *x*-axis and *y*-axis cross at the point (0, 0). This point is called the origin.

| Example 1 | Name the coordinates of the points *A*, *B*, and *C*. |
| --- | --- |

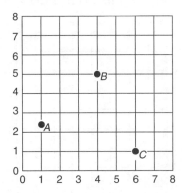

## Solution:

*A* (2, 2), *B* (4, 5), *C* (6, 1)

| **Example 2** | If a square is drawn on a coordinate axis and three of the coordinates of the vertices of the square are *A* (2, 4), *B* (5, 4), *C* (5, 7), what are the coordinates of the fourth vertex *D*? |

## Solution:

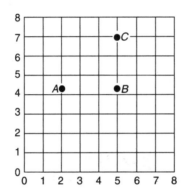

Since the figure is a square, the fourth vertex must be in line with points *A* and *C*. So, point *D* has the coordinates (2, 7).

## Lesson Practice

For questions 1–4, plot the following points on the coordinate axis below.

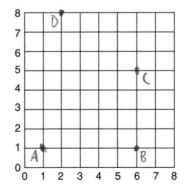

1.  *A* (1, 1)

2.  *B* (6, 1)

3.  *C* (6, 5)

4.  *D* (2, 8)

5.  What figure is produced if the points in questions 1–4 are connected by line segments *AB, BC, CD,* and *DA*?

*Trapezoid* ✗

*Quadrilateral*

## Test Preparation Practice

Circle the letter of the correct answer.

For questions 1–4, use the coordinate axis below.

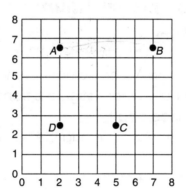

1.  What are the coordinates of point *A*?

    A.  (2, 2)

    B.  (5, 2)

    C.  (7, 6)

    D.  (2, 6)

2.  How long is line segment *AB*?

    A.  4

    B.  3

    C.  5

    D.  8

3. If line segments *AB, BC, CD,* and *AD* are drawn, what kind of figure is created?

   A. parallelogram

   B. square

   C. triangle

   D. trapezoid

4. Which line segment is the shortest?

   A. *AB*

   B. *BC*

   C. *CD*

   D. *DA*

## Mapping a Figure onto Another Figure Through Transformations

We can move shapes or figures on the coordinate plane. A translation slides a figure horizontally, vertically, or diagonally. When a figure is translated, all of the points in the figure maintain the same distance apart.

A figure can also be transformed by flipping the figure over a line. This is called a reflection.

A rotation is a transformation where the figure is turned around a point.

**Example 1** | **Draw what the figure would look like if it were rotated one-half turn around point _E_.**

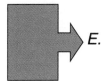

## Solution:

We turn the figure around point *E.*

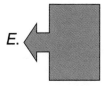

## Example 2

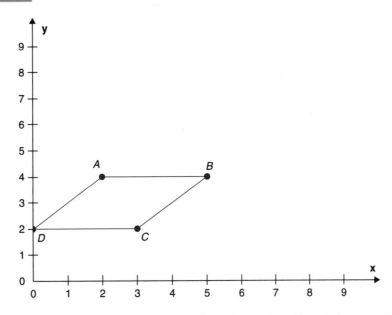

If parallelogram *ABCD* is translated up 2 units and to the right 3 units, what are the coordinates of the vertices of the new parallelogram *A'B'C'D'*?

## Solution:

Point *A* was originally (2, 4), so to move the point up 2 and right 3, we add 2 units to the *y*-coordinate and 3 units to the *x*-coordinate. *A'* is (5, 6).

Similarly, *B* moves from (5, 4) to *B'* at (8,6), *C* moves from (3, 2) to *C'* at (6, 4), and *D* moves from (0, 2) to *D'* at (3,4).

## Example 3   **If the following trapezoid is reflected over a vertical line, what does the reflected shape look like?**

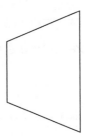

## Solution:

When we reflect, we flip the figure over the line of reflection.

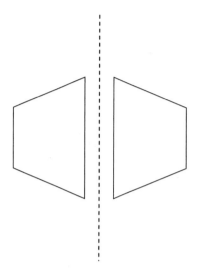

 **Lesson Practice**

For questions 1–4, draw the figure after the described transformation.

1.   Rotate the triangle one-half turn around point *C*.

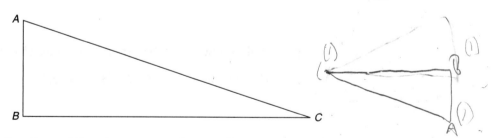

2.   Draw the reflection of the figure over the vertical line.

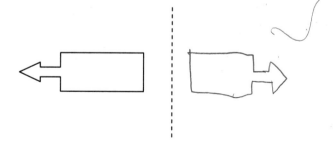

3. Draw the new parallelogram if parallelogram *ABCD* is translated right 2 units and down 3 units.

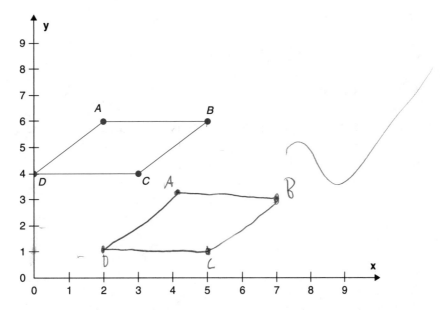

4. Draw the new rectangle if rectangle *RSTU* is rotated one-half turn about point *S*.

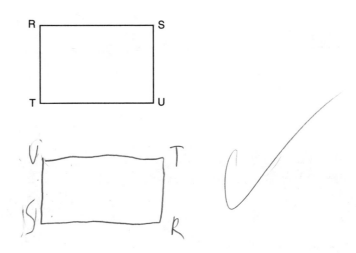

## Test Preparation Practice

Circle the letter of the correct answer.

1. Which of the following represents the triangle after it has been reflected over side *BC*?

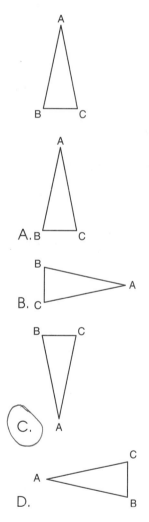

**2.** What kind of transformation produces the following?

Original                    After the Transformation

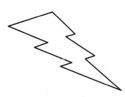 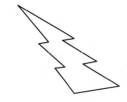

   A.   reflection over a vertical line

   B.   reflection over a horizontal line

   C.   rotation of one-half turn

   D.   no transformation

# Chapter 7—Solutions

## Creating Geometric Shapes with Given Parameters

**Lesson Practice**

1. – 4.

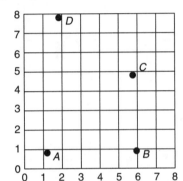

5. quadrilateral

**Test Preparation Practice**

1. D
2. C
3. D
4. C

## Mapping a Figure onto Another Figure Through Transformations

**Lesson Practice**

1.

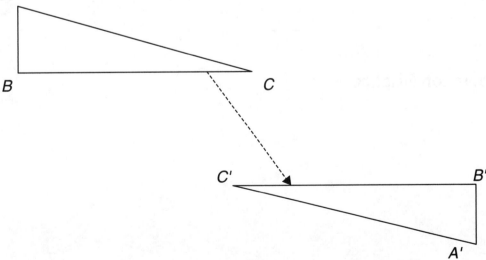

2.

3.

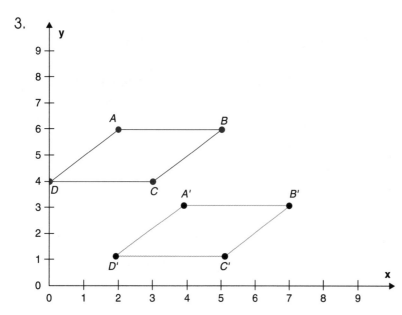

4.

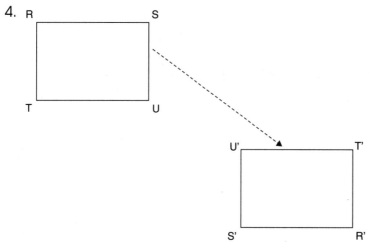

## Test Preparation Practice

1. C
2. C

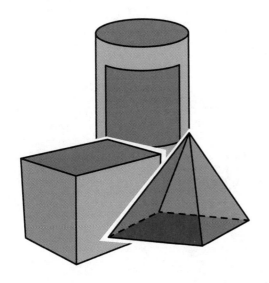

# Chapter 8
# Units of Measurement

## Converting Between Units of Measure in the Metric System

It is important to be able to convert between different units of measure. When we use the metric system, we use the following conversions to measure length, mass, and capacity.

| Metric Units of Length | Meter (m) | Example |
|---|---|---|
| 1 Kilometer (km) = | 1000 meters (m) | 1 km ≈ 10 football fields |
| 1 meter (m) = | 100 centimeters (cm) | 1 m ≈ Width of a refrigerator |
| 1 centimeter (cm) = | 10 millimeters (mm) | 1 cm ≈ Width of a human finger |
| Metric Units of Capacity | Liter (L) | |
| 1 Kiloliter (kL) = | 1000 liters (L) | |
| 1 liter (L) = | 100 centiliters (cL) | 1 L ≈ pitcher of water |
| 1 centiliter (cL) = | 10 milliliters (mL) | 1 mL ≈ one drop from an eye dropper |
| Metric Units of Mass | Gram (g) | |
| 1 Kilogram (kg) = | 1,000 grams (g) | 1 kg ≈ 1 textbook |
| 1 gram (g) = | 100 centigrams (cg) | 1 g ≈ paperclip |
| 1 centigram (cg) = | 10 milligram (mg) | |

To change from a larger quantity to a smaller quantity, we multiply.
To change from a smaller quantity to a larger quantity, we divide.

**Example 1**  **Convert 4600 grams to kilograms.**

## Solution:

Since grams are smaller than kilograms, we will divide.
1000 g = 1 kg
4600 g = 4600 ÷ 1000 = 4.6 kg.

**Example 2**  **Convert 3 km to meters.**

## Solution:

Since km are larger than meters, we multiply.
1 km = 1000 m
3 km = 3 × 1000 = 3000 m

**Example 3**  **If Dave is 1.6 m tall, and Jim is 134 cm tall, how many centimeters taller is Dave than Jim?**

## Solution:

We need to convert Dave's height into cm. 1.6 m = 1.6 × 100 = 160 cm.
So, Dave is 160 − 134 = 26 cm taller than Jim.

## Lesson Practice

For questions 1–4, fill-in-the-blank to complete the conversion.

1.  86 mm = _8.6_ cm

2.  286 cl = _2.86_ l

3. 45 kg = __450,000__ cg

4. 0.007 km = __7__ m

5. If Jackie weighs 65 kg and Thomas weighs 80000 g, how many more grams does Thomas weigh than Jackie? __15,000__

6. If a bucket can hold 20 liters of water, how many milliliters could 3 buckets hold? __60,000__

## Test Preparation Practice

Circle the letter of the correct answer.

1. About how many mL would a glass of milk hold?

    A.  5

    B.  50

    C.  500

    D.  5000

2. Which symbol makes the statement true?
   85 g _____ 850 mg

    A.  >

    B.  <

    C.  =

    D.  none of the above

3. An average car weighs approximately

    A.  1000 mg

    B.  1000 cg

    C.  1000 g

    D.  1000 kg

4.   A full-grown snake is about how long?

   A.   10 mm

   B.   10 cm

   C.   1 m

   D.   10 km

## Converting Between Units of Measure in the Customary System

When using the customary system of measurement, we use the following units.

| Length | Miles (mi), yards (yd), feet (ft), inches (in) | Example |
|---|---|---|
| 1 mile = | 1760 yd. | 15 football fields |
| 1 yard = | 3 ft. | Length from top of head to waist of an adult |
| 1 foot = | 12 inches | Length of an adult foot |
| 1 mile = | 5,280 feet | |
| **Weight** | **Pounds (lb), Ounces (oz), tons (T)** | |
| 1 ton = | 2,000 lbs. | Small car |
| 1 pound = | 16 oz | Box of cereal |
| **Capacity** | **fluid ounce (fl oz), cup (c), pint (pt), quart (qt), gallon (gal)** | |
| 1 gallon = | 4 quarts | Large container of milk |
| 1 quart = | 2 pints | Large container of berries |
| 1 pint = | 2 cups | Jar of peanut butter |
| 1 cup = | 8 fl oz | Cup of hot chocolate |
| 1 fl oz. | | One spoonful of cold medicine |

To change from a larger quantity to a smaller quantity, we multiply.
To change from a smaller quantity to a larger quantity, we divide.

**Example 1**  **Convert 10 pounds to ounces.**

## Solution:

Since pounds are larger than ounces, we will multiply.
    1 lb = 16 ounces
    10 lbs = 16 × 10 = 160 oz

**Example 2**  **Convert 3 miles to feet.**

## Solution:

Since miles are larger than feet, we multiply.
    1 mi = 5280 ft
    3 mi = 3 × 5280 = 15,840 ft

**Example 3**  **If Dave is 2.1 yds tall, and Jim is 5 ft tall, how many feet taller is Dave than Jim?**

## Solution:

We need to convert Dave's height into ft. 2.1 yds = 2.1 ×3 = 6.3 ft.
    So, Dave is 6.3 – 5 = 1.3 feet taller than Jim.

## Lesson Practice

For questions 1–4, fill in the blank to complete the conversion.

1.  6 ft = _72_ in

2.  286 lbs = _0.143_ tons

3.  4.5 gal = _18_ quarts

4.  36 inches = _3_ ft

5. If Jackie drinks 1 pint of coffee and Thomas drinks 3 cups of hot chocolate, how many more fluid ounces of hot chocolate did Thomas drink than Jackie drank of coffee? ___8 fl. oz.___ ✓

6. If a bucket can hold 5 gallons of water, how many quarts of water does the bucket hold? ___20 quarts___ ✓

## Test Preparation Practice

Circle the letter of the correct answer.

1. About how many pounds would a 3-ton truck weigh?

   A. 3 lbs.

   B. 300 lbs.

   C. 3000 lbs.

   (D.) 6000 lbs.

2. Which symbol makes the statement true?
   5 gal _____ 30 quarts

   A. >

   (B.) <

   C. =

   D. none of the above

3. About how long is a swimming pool?

   (A.) 25 feet

   B. 25 yards

   C. 25 miles

   D. 25 inches

4. A full-grown tiger weighs approximately

   A. 5 lbs.

   B. 500 ounces

   C. 500 tons

   D. 500 lbs.

# Choosing Appropriate Units to Measure Geometric Quantities

When we measure quantities, it is important to choose the correct units of measure.

| Quantity | Customary Units | Metric Units |
|---|---|---|
| Length (distance) | Feet (ft), Inches (in), Miles (mi) | Meters (m), Kilometers (km), Centimeters (cm) |
| Angles | Degrees (°) | Degrees (°) |
| Area | Square units—for example, square ft, square in. | Square units—for example, square m, square km, square cm |
| Surface Area | Square units—for example, square ft, square in. | Square units—for example, square m, square km, square cm |
| Volume of solids and gases | Cubic units—for example, cubic ft, cubic in. | Cubic units—for example, cubic m, cubic km, cubic cm |
| Volume of Liquids (capacity) | Gallons (gal), ounces (oz) | Liters (L), Kiloliters (kL), centiliters (cL) |

**Example 1** **If we wish to measure how far apart the state of New Jersey and the state of California are, what units of measurement would be most appropriate?**

## Solution:

Since New Jersey and California are a long distance apart, appropriate units would be either miles of kilometers.

**Example 2**    **What units should be used to measure the volume of water in a bathtub?**

## Solution:

Since water is a liquid, the appropriate units of measurement would be gallons or liters.

**Example 3**    **If a scale on a map shows that 3 inches on the map is the equivalent to 100 miles, about how many miles apart are two cities that are about 9 inches apart on a map?**

## Solution:

Since 3 in. = 100 miles, we set up a proportion of $\frac{3}{9} = \frac{100}{x}$ and then solve for $x$. Solve by cross-multiplying. $3x = 900$

$$\frac{3x}{3} = \frac{900}{3}$$

$$x = 300 \text{ miles}$$

**Example 4**    **What unit of measurement should be used to measure the amount of carpet needed to cover a floor?**

## Solution:

Since covering a floor is area, we need to use either square feet or square meters.

## Lesson Practice

1. What metric units should be used to measure the length of a paper clip?

   cm ✓

2. What customary units would be used to measure the height of a man?

   feet ✓

3.  What metric units would be used measure the volume of the helium in a balloon? _____ cm³ _____

4.  What customary units are most likely to be used in the scale of length on a globe? _____ in. _____

## Test Preparation Practice

Circle the letter of the correct answer.

1.  Which of the following should be used to measure the length of a dog?

    A.  lbs

    B.  inches

    C.  tons

    D.  gallons

2.  Which of the following are the metric units that would be used to measure the amount of water in a swimming pool?

    A.  cL

    B.  gallons

    C.  kL

    D.  km

3.  What units should be used to determine how much paint should be bought to paint a barn?

    A.  liters

    B.  square feet

    C.  square miles

    D.  cubic yards

4.  What should be used to determine how much gasoline a gas tank can hold?

A.  meters

B.  cubic feet

C.  grams

D.  cubic grams

## Converting Between Metric and Customary Units of Measure

We use the following conversions to estimate length, weight, and capacity.

| Length | 1 km ≈ 0.6 mi. |
|--------|----------------|
|        | 1 m ≈ 1.1 yd. |
|        | 1 cm ≈ 0.4 in. |
| Weight | 1 kg ≈ 2.2 lbs. |
| Capacity | 1 L ≈ 1 qt. The quart is slightly smaller than the liter. |

**Example 1**    **In the Olympics, men throw a 2 kg discus, about how many pounds does the discus weigh?**

## Solution:

Since 1 kg ≈ 2.2 lbs, then 2 kg ≈ 2 × 2.2 = 4.4 lbs.

**Example 2**    **How many kilometers long is a trip that measures 100 miles?**

## Solution:

If 1 km = 0.6 mi. we need to divide 100 miles by 0.6 miles. So, 100 ÷ 0.6 = 166.7 km.

| **Example 3** | About how many meters tall is a mirror that measures 60 inches tall? |

## Solution:

First, we need to convert inches into yards. Since there are 12 inches in one foot and 3 feet in one yard, that means that there are 12 × 3 = 36 inches in one yard. So, 60 inches = 60 ÷ 36 = 1.7 yards. Since 1 meter is slightly larger than that 1 yard, we can say that 60 inches is approximately 1.5 meters.

| **Example 4** | About how many liters is a 16 oz. can of soda? |

## Solution:

16 oz. = 2 cups. So, 16 oz = 1 pint, and since 2 pints = 1 quart, we say that
16 oz. = 0.5 quarts. Thus, a 16 oz. can of soda is approximately one-half of a liter.

| **Example 5** | If 10 inches of snow is equal to 1 inch of rain, about how much rain should we expect if 50 inches of snow are forecast, but the temperature warmed up above freezing and it rained instead of snowed? |

## Solution:

Since 10 inches of snow = 1 in of rain, 50 inches of snow = 5 × 1 = 5 inches of rain.

| **Example 6** | If Jason sleeps 7 hours per day, how many hours did he sleep during one week? |

## Solution:

Since there are 7 days in a week, Jason sleeps 7 × 7 = 49 hours per week.

## Lesson Practice

For questions 1–8, circle the larger quantity.

1. 15 m or 2 mi
2. 30 g or 10 pounds
3. 3 mi or 6 km
4. 100 cm or 75 inches
5. 10 L or 2 gal
6. 10 m or 30 feet
7. 3 tons or 50 kg
8. 1600 oz. or 1 ton

## Test Preparation Practice

Circle the letter of the correct answer.

1. What would be a reasonable estimate for the weight of a couch?

   A. 50 ounces

   B. 50 pounds

   C. 50 grams

   D. 50 tons

2. If hair grows about 0.25 inches per month, how long will hair grow during one year?

   A. 1 inches

   B. 3 inches

   C. 10 inches

   D. 1 foot

3. Which object holds about 130 fluid ounces?

   A. coffee cup

   B. bottle of ketchup

   C. milk jug

   D. gas tank

4. Which of the following is the smallest?

   A. 1 gallon

   B. 10 liters

   C. 500 mL

   D. 50 quarts

# Chapter 8—Solutions

## Converting Between Units of Measure in the Metric System

### Lesson Practice

1. 8.6
2. 2.86
3. 4,500,000
4. 7
5. 15,000
6. 60,000

### Test Preparation Practice

1. C
2. A
3. D
4. C

## Converting Between Units of Measure in the Customary System

### Lesson Practice

1. 72
2. 0.143
3. 18
4. 3
5. 8
6. 20

### Test Preparation Practice

1. D
2. B
3. B
4. D

## Choosing Appropriate Units to Measure Geometric Quantities

### Lesson Practice

1. mm or cm
2. feet
3. cubic meters
4. miles

### Test Preparation Practice

1. B
2. C
3. B
4. B

# Converting Between Metric and Customary Units of Measure

## Lesson Practice

1. 2 mi
2. 10 pounds
3. 6 km
4. 75 inches
5. 10 L
6. 10 m
7. 3 tons
8. 1 ton

## Test Preparation Practice

1. B
2. B
3. C
4. C

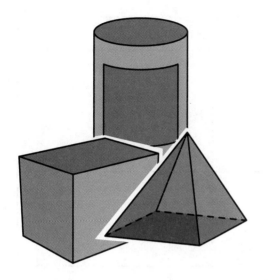

# Chapter 9
# Measuring Geometric Objects

## Finding the Perimeter and Area of Various Geometric Figures

Perimeter (*P*) is the distance around an object. Area (*A*) is the number of square units necessary to cover the object, such as painting a wall. To find the perimeter or area of geometric figures, we use various formulas.

| Shape | Perimeter | Area |
|---|---|---|
| Triangle | The sum of the lengths of all three sides of the triangle. | $A = \frac{1}{2}bh$ |
| Parallelogram | $P = 2l + 2b$ | $A = bh$ |
| Rectangle | $P = 2l + 2w$ | $A = lw$ |
| Square | $P = 4s$ | $A = s^2$ |
| Trapezoid | $P =$ the sum of the lengths of the sides of the trapezoid | $A = = \frac{1}{2}(a + b)h$ |
| Circle | The perimeter of a circle is called the circumference ($C$ of the circle). $C = 2\pi r$ or $C = \pi d$ | $A = \pi r^2$ |

**Example 1**    Find the perimeter and area of the rectangle below.

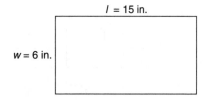

## Solution:

$P = 2l + 2w = 2(15) + 2(6) = 30 + 12 = 42$ inches.
$A = l\,w = (15)\,(6) = 90$ in.$^2$

**Example 2**    If a circle has a diameter of 6 feet. Find the circumference and area of the circle.

## Solution:

$C = \pi d = (3.14)(6) = 18.84$ ft.
To find the area, we have to find the radius. Since the radius is one-half the distance of a diameter, the radius is equal to $6 \div 2 = 3$. So, $A = \pi r^2 = (3.14)(3)^2 = 28.26$ ft$^2$.

**Example 3**    On the grid below, each square represents one square unit. Find the area of the irregular shape drawn on the grid.

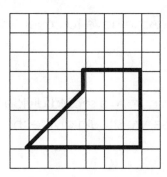

## Solution:

To estimate the area of the irregular figure, count the number of squares within the shape.

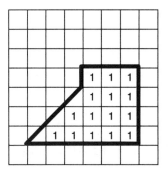

There are 15 squares within the shape. There are three one-half squares that we have not counted yet. So, the area is 15 + 3(1/2) = 15 + 1.5 = 16.5 square units.

**Example 4**    **Alice wants to paint a wall. The wall has the following shape and dimensions.**

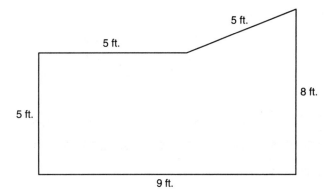

How many square feet does Alice have to cover with paint?

## Solution:

To find the area of this irregular figure, we should divide the region into several shapes that we know. In this case, we should divide the region into a rectangle and a triangle.

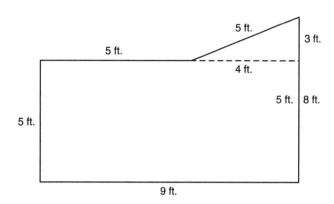

The area of the rectangle is $A = (9)(5) = 45$ ft.$^2$ The area of the triangle is $A = (0.5)(4)(3) = 6$ ft.$^2$. So, the area of the entire region is $45 + 6 = 51$ ft.$^2$.

**Example 5**    Using the same figure in Example 4, what would be the perimeter of the wall?

## Solution:

$P = 5 + 5 + 5 + 8 + 9 = 32$ ft.

## Lesson Practice

For questions 1–4, find the perimeter and area of each figure.

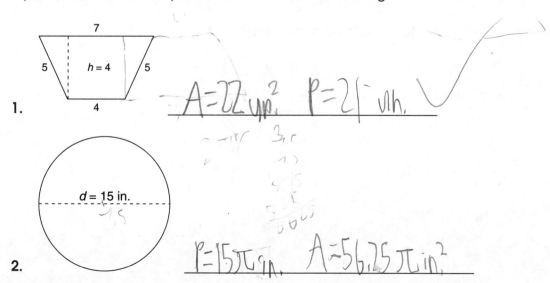

1.    $A = 22 \text{ yd}^2$    $P = 21$ vlh.

2.    $P = 15\pi$ in.    $A = 56.25\pi$ in$^2$

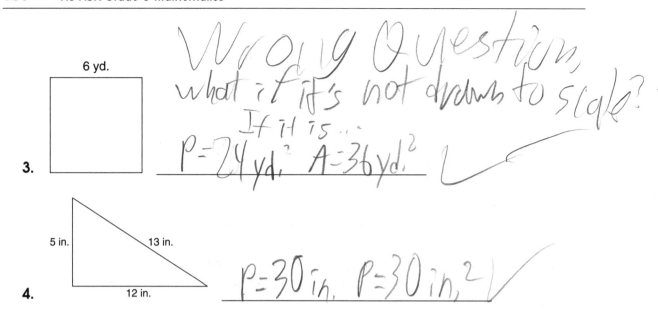

6 yd.

3.

*Wrong Question, what if it's not drawn to scale?*
*If it is...*
$P = 24$ yd. $A = 36$ yd.$^2$

4.

5 in.   13 in.

12 in.

$P = 30$ in, $P = 30$ in,$^2$

## Test Preparation Practice

Circle the letter of the correct answer.

1.  Which answer is the best estimate of the area of a circle with a radius 4 cm?

    A.  12 cm$^2$

    B.  25 cm$^2$

    C.  40 cm$^2$

    D.  50 cm$^2$

Questions 2 and 3 refer to the following rhombus.

7.5 mm

7 mm

2. What is the perimeter of the rhombus?

   A.  20 mm

   B.  67.5 mm

   C.  30 mm

   D.  33 mm

3. What is the area of the rhombus?

   A.  20 mm²

   B.  52.5 mm²

   C.  30 mm²

   D.  33 mm²

Question 4 refers to the following figure.

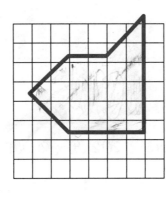

4. What is the area of the figure?

   A.  16 square units

   B.  20 square units

   C.  22 square units

   D.  24 square units

## Surface Area and Volume of Rectangular Prisms and Cylinders

We use formulas to find the surface area and volume of three-dimensional figures.

| Figure | Surface Area | Volume |
|---|---|---|
| Rectangular Prism | $SA = 2lw + 2lh + 2wh$ | $V = lwh$ |
| Cylinder | $SA = 2\pi r^2 + 2\pi rh$ | $V = \pi r^2 h$ |

**Example 1**    Find the surface area and volume of the box below.

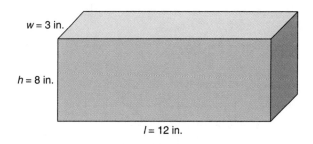

$w = 3$ in.

$h = 8$ in.

$l = 12$ in.

### Solution:

$SA = 2lw + 2lh + 2wh = 2(12)(3) + 2(12)(8) + 2(3)(8) = 72 + 192 + 48 = 312$ in². 
$V = l\,w\,h = (12)(3)(8) = 288$ in³.

**Example 2**    Find the surface area and volume of the cylinder below.

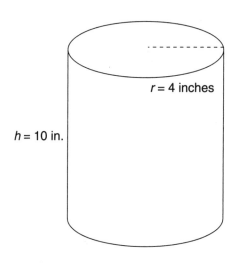

$r = 4$ inches

$h = 10$ in.

## Solution:

$SA = 2\pi r^2 + 2\pi rh = 2(3.14)(4^2) + 2(3.14)(4)(10) = 351.68 \text{ in}^2$

$V = \pi r^2 h = (3.14)(4^2)(10) = 502.4 \text{ in}^3$

## Lesson Practice

Questions 1 and 2 refer to the cylinder below.

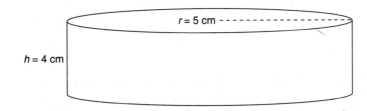

$r = 5 \text{ cm}$

$h = 4 \text{ cm}$

1.  Find the volume of the cylinder. ____ $100\pi \text{ cm}^3$ ✓ ____
2.  Find the surface area of the cylinder. ____ $90\pi \text{ cm}^2$ ✓ ____

Questions 3 and 4 refer to the box below.

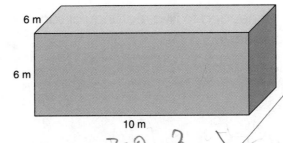

6 m

6 m

10 m

3.  Find the volume of the box. ____ $360 \text{ m}^3$ ✓ ____
4.  Find the surface area of the box. ____ $312 \text{ m}^2$ ✓ ____

## Test Preparation Practice

Circle the letter of the correct answer.

1.  About how much water would a cylindrical pitcher with a radius of 3 inches and a height of 10 inches hold?

    A.  90 cubic inches

    B.  270 cubic inches

    C.  1000 cubic inches

    D.  3000 cubic inches

2.  How much paint is needed to paint the outside of rectangular chest of drawers that is 5 feet high, 4 feet wide, and 2 feet deep?

    A.  40 square feet

    B.  11 square feet

    C.  76 square feet

    D.  100 square feet

3.  How much sand is needed to fill a rectangular sand box that is 6 inches deep, 5 feet wide, and 5 feet long?

    A.  150 cubic feet

    B.  16 cubic feet

    C.  12.5 cubic feet

    D.  25 cubic feet

4.  If wrapping paper costs $0.50 per square foot, how much would it cost to wrap a cube that is 2 feet tall?

    A.  $12.00

    B.  $14.00

    C.  $16.00

    D.  $20.00

# Chapter 9—Solutions

## Finding the Perimeter and Area of Various Geometric Figures

### Lesson Practice

1. $P = 21, A = 22$
2. $P = 47.12$ in., $A = 176.71$ square inches
3. $P = 24$ yd., $A = 36$ square yards
4. $P = 30$ in., $A = 30$ square inches

### Test Preparation Practice

1. D
2. C
3. B
4. C

## Surface Area and Volume of Rectangular Prisms and Cylinders

### Lesson Practice

1. 314.16 cubic centimeters
2. 282.74 square centimeters
3. 360 cubic meters
4. 312 square meters

### Test Preparation Practice

1. B
2. C
3. C
4. A

# Unit III

## Patterns and Algebra

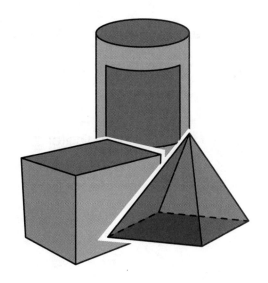

# Chapter 10
# Patterns

## Solving Problems and Making Predictions from Patterns Composed of Whole and Rational Numbers

Patterns are sequences that follow a rule or formula. Often times we are asked to make predictions based on patterns and sequences of numbers.

| Example 1 | Describe the rule that produces the following pattern and then predict the next three numbers. 3, 6, 9, 12, ... |
|---|---|

**Solution:**

Every number is the previous number plus 3. Thus, the rule is to add 3. The next three numbers are $12 + 3 = 15$, and $15 + 3 = 18$, and $18 + 3 = 21$.

| Example 2 | What would be the 7th number in the following sequence? $\frac{1}{2}, 1, \frac{3}{2}, 2, \frac{5}{2}, ...$ |
|---|---|

**Solution:**

The rule is to add $\frac{1}{2}$ to the previous number, thus, the sixth number is

3 and the seventh number is $\frac{7}{2}$.

**Example 3**    Write the pattern rule and the next two numbers for the following sequence. $\dfrac{5}{9}, \dfrac{7}{11}, \dfrac{9}{13}, \ldots$

## Solution:

The rule is to add two to each numerator and to add two to each denominator.

Thus, the next two numbers are $\dfrac{11}{15}, \dfrac{13}{17}$.

## Lesson Practice

In questions 1–4, write the rule for the pattern and find the next two numbers.

1. 5, 15, 45, … _X3 / 135, 405_ ✓

2. 4, 9, 16, 25, … _square next consecutive #/36, 49_ ✓

3. 81, 27, 9, … _÷3 / 3, 1_ ✓

4. 1, −2, 4, −8, 16, … _X(-2) / -32, 64_ ✓

5. If a bacteria population doubles every day, the population of the bacteria follows the table displayed below.

| Day | Bacteria Population |
|-----|---------------------|
| 1 | 1 |
| 2 | 2 |
| 3 | 4 |
| 4 | 8 |
| 5 | 16 |

What will be the population of the bacteria on day 8? _128_ ✓

6. If a football team runs 10 sprints at the end of practice and the lengths of the sprints are given by the following pattern, how long will the 10th sprint be? 15, 20, 25, 30, … _60_ ✓

## Test Preparation Practice

Circle the letter of the correct answer.

1. Which number correctly fills in the blank in the following pattern?
   3, 7, 11, ____, 19, 23

   A. 12

   B. 13

   C. 14

   D. 15

2. What rule describes the following pattern?
   100, 200, 400, 800, ...

   A. multiply by 2

   B. add 100

   C. dividing by 2

   D. squaring

3. What rule describes the following pattern?
   50, 5, 0.5, 0.05, 0.005

   A. dividing by 5

   B. dividing by 1

   C. multiplying by 10

   D. dividing by 10

4. An ice cream shop finds that during the month of July, the number of ice cream cones that it sells increases by 10 each day for the entire month. If on July 11th, the ice cream shop sells 35 ice cream cones, how many ice cream cones will they sell on July 15th?

   A. 45                          C. 65

   B. 55                          D. 75

## Creating Patterns and Making Predictions from Tables, Equations, and Graphs

We can make predictions based on visual representations of patterns as well.

**Example 1**

**What will be the next shape in the pattern?**

## Solution:

Since each shape repeats every third shape, the next shape will be a smiley face; also, since every other shape is shaded grey, the smiley face will not be shaded.

Thus, the next shape is

**Example 2** **Given the following pattern, how many blocks will be in the 4th figure in the sequence?**

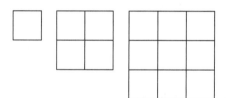

## Solution:

The number of blocks is the sequence 1, 4, 9, ..., thus, the next number is the next squared number, which is 16. This can be found by viewing 1, 4, 9, as $1^2$, $2^2$, $3^2$, ... or by drawing the next figure in the sequence.

**Example 3** **The graph below shows the average salary of professional players for the past 35 years. What would be a reasonable estimate of the average salary of a player in 2010?**

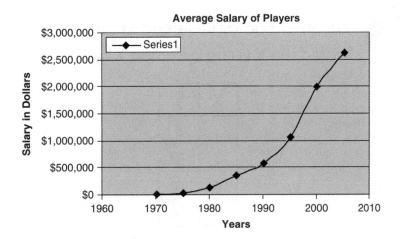

## Solution:

By extending the line in the graph, it appears that the average player salary will be about $3,250,000.

**Example 4**    **The following line graph shows the value of Company A.**

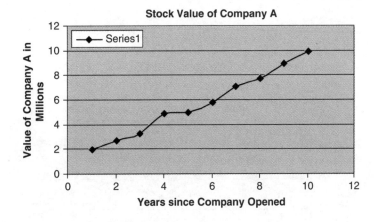

About how much, in millions, will Company A be worth 12 years after it opened according to this model?

## Solution:

By extending the graph, it appears that the value of Company A in year 12 will be about 12 million dollars.

| **Example 5** | Given the data presented in the table below, what would the Y value be when X = 8? |

| X | Y |
|---|---|
| 2 | 8 |
| 3 | 10 |
| 4 | 12 |
| 5 | 14 |

## Solution:

Since the pattern indicates that as X increases by one, Y increases by 2, when X is 6, Y is 16, when X is 7, Y is 18, and then when X is 8, Y is 20.

## Lesson Practice

For questions 1–4, use the following graph to make accurate predictions.

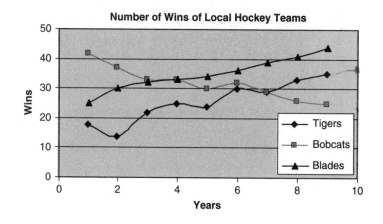

Number of Wins of Local Hockey Teams

1. How many wins does the model predict that the Tigers will have in Year 10?
   _37 wins_ ✓

2. How many wins does the model predict that the Bobcats will have in Year 10?
   _23 wins_ ✓

3. How many wins does the model predict that the Blades will have in Year 10?
   _46 wins_ ✓

4. What is the approximate difference in wins between the Blades and Bobcats in Year 10? _13 wins_ ✗ _23_

## Test Preparation Practice

Circle the letter of the correct answer.
Questions 1, 2, and 3 refer to the graph below.

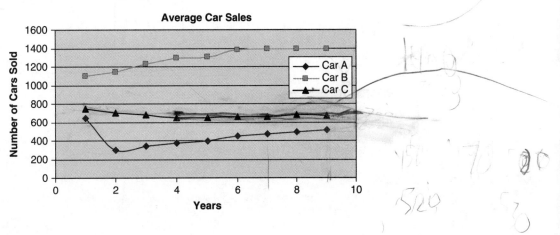

1. About how many more cars of brand B will be sold in year 10 than will be sold of brand A?

   A. 300

   B. 500

   C. 700

   D. 900

2.  Approximately how many cars of Brand C will be sold in Year 10?

    A.  200

    B.  400

    C.  600

    D.  700

3.  About how many cars total will be sold in Year 10?

    A.  2000

    B.  2300

    C.  2600

    D.  3000

4.  Given the data in the chart, predict the value of Y when X = 21.

| X | Y |
|----|----|
| 12 | 25 |
| 15 | 31 |
| 18 | 37 |

    A.  40

    B.  43

    C.  46

    D.  49

## Patterns and Recursive Formulas

Patterns that are created by using the previous numbers in a pattern are called Recursive Patterns. For example, 3, 4, 7, 11, 18, 39,... is a recursive pattern because each successive number after the first two is the sum of the previous two numbers. In this case, 7 = 3 + 4, 11 = 7 + 4, and so on.

There are two particularly well-known recursive sequences, (1) the Fibonacci Sequence, and (2) Pascal's Triangle.

The Fibonacci Sequence starts with two successive 1's, and the remaining numbers are found by adding the two previous numbers.

**Example 1**    **Write the first 10 numbers in the Fibonacci sequence.**

## Solution:

1, 1, 2, 3, 5, 8, 13, 21, 34, 55
To create the Fibonacci Sequence, we start with two 1's, and then add the two previous numbers to create the next entry. Thus, 1 + 1 = 2, 1 + 2 = 3, 2 + 3 = 5, 3 + 5 = 8, 5 + 8 = 13, 8 + 13 = 21, 13 + 21 = 34, 21 + 34 = 55.

Pascal's Triangle is a triangle with 1's on the outer diagonals. Every number in between is the sum of the two numbers diagonally above it.

```
Row 0:                        1
Row 1:                    1       1
Row 2:                1       2       1
Row 3:            1       3       3       1
Row 4:        1       4       6       4       1
Row 5:    1       5       10      10      5       1
```

**Example 2**    **If you start in the diagonal of Row 2, what would the 5th number in the diagonal be?**

## Solution:

The diagonal of Row 2 is the sequence 1, 3, 6, 10. 1 increased by 2, 3 increased by 3, 6 increased by 4, thus 10 will increase by 5 and the next number in the sequence is 15.

| Example 3 | If a sequence is produced by multiplying the previous two numbers and the first two numbers are 1 and 2, what would be the fifth number? |

## Solution:

$1 \times 2 = 2$
$2 \times 2 = 4$
$2 \times 4 = 8$

Thus, the sequence would be 1, 2, 2, 4, 8 and the fifth number is 8.

## Lesson Practice

1.  Construct the first 6 Rows of Pascal's Triangle.

1
1 2 1
1 3 3 1
1 4 6 4 1
1 5 10 10 5 1

## Test Preparation Practice

Circle the letter of the correct answer.

1. Which of the following is a Fibonacci number?

   A. 0

   B. 4

   C. 8

   D. 10

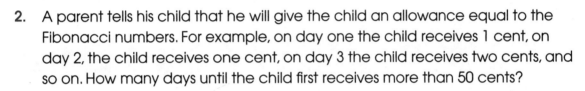

2. A parent tells his child that he will give the child an allowance equal to the Fibonacci numbers. For example, on day one the child receives 1 cent, on day 2, the child receives one cent, on day 3 the child receives two cents, and so on. How many days until the child first receives more than 50 cents?

   A. 5

   B. 8

   C. 10

   D. 12

3. If a new triangle was formed that followed the same rule as Pascal's Triangle and one of the row's of this new triangle was 2, 8, 12, 8, 2. What would be the previous row?

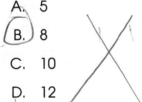

   A. 2, 6, 6, 2

   B. 1, 3, 3, 1

   C. 2, 10, 20, 20, 10, 2

   D. 1, 5, 5, 1

4. If the first diagonal of Pascal's Triangle is the diagonal row of 1's, what would be the second diagonal row of Pascal's triangle?

   A. 1, 2, 3, 4, …

   B. 1, 3, 5, 7, …

   C. 1, 4, 7, 10, …

   D. 1, 5, 9, 13, …

# Chapter 10—Solutions

## Solving Problems and Making Predictions from Patterns Composed of Whole and Rational Numbers

### Lesson Practice

1. Multiply by 3, 135, and 405
2. Square the number, $6^2 = 36$, $7^2 = 49$
3. Divide by 3, 3, 1
4. Multiply by $-2$. $-32, 64$
5. 128
6. 60

### Test Preparation Practice

1. D
2. A
3. D
4. D

## Creating Patterns and Making Predictions from Tables, Equations, and Graphs

### Lesson Practice

1. 40
2. 22
3. 48
4. 26

### Test Preparation Practice

1. D
2. D
3. C
4. B

## Patterns and Recursive Formulas

**Lesson Practice**

1.
```
                    1
                1       1
            1       2       1
        1       3       3       1
      1     4       6       4     1
    1     5    10       10     5     1
```

**Test Preparation Practice**

1. C
2. C
3. A
4. A

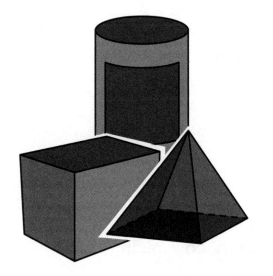

# Chapter 11
## Procedures, Functions, and Relationships

### Evaluating Numerical and Algebraic Expressions

An algebraic expression is a math statement that involves numbers, variables and operations. Variables are usually letters that can represent many different numbers. If we know the number that the variable represents, we can substitute that number for the variable. The algebraic expression is now a numerical expression and should be evaluated using the established order of operations (parentheses, exponents, multiplication or division, addition or subtraction).

**Example 1**    **Evaluate the expression if $a = 3$.**

$2a + (6 + a)^2 \div 3$

### Solution:

We substitute 3 in for $a$ in the expression and then follow the order of operations.

$2a + (6 + a)^2 \div 3 = 2(3) + (6 + 3)^2 \div 3 = 2(3) + 9^2 \div 3 = 2(3) + 81 \div 3 =$
$6 + 81 \div 3 = 6 + 27 = 33$

We can write algebraic expressions that describe real-life situations.

| **Example 2** | Dave drove 20 miles further than Jamie drove. If Jamie drove $j$ miles, write an expression that describes how far Dave drove. |

## Solution:

Dave drove $j + 20$ miles.

| **Example 3** | If a new car costs twice as much as a used car, and a used car costs $C$ dollars, how much would a new car cost? |

## Solution:

A new car would cost $2C$, because twice implies that we must multiply by two.

## Lesson Practice

For questions 1–4, evaluate the expression by substituting the correct value.

1. $3x - 14 \div 2x, x = 7$ _____ 20 ✓

2. $\dfrac{(3c - 10)}{5}, c = 20$ _____ 10 ✓

3. $5 + d \div 8 + 2d, d = 24$ _____ 56 ✓

4. $56 - (2 + x)^2, x = 5$ _____ 7 ✓

For questions 5 and 6, write an algebraic expression that describes the given situation.

5. Keri has three times as many dolls as Jill. If Jill has $j$ dolls, how many dolls does Keri have? ___ $k = 3j$ ✗

6. Davis threw 14 more pitches than Jackson threw. If Jackson threw $J$ pitches, how many pitches did Davis throw? ___ $j + 14 = d$ ✓

## Test Preparation Practice

Circle the letter of the correct answer.

1. What is the value of $x^2 - (x + 4)$ if $x = 4$?

   A. 16

   B. 8

   C. 20

   D. 4

2. Which of the following is the largest if $z = 3$?

   A. $z - 3$

   B. $z + 3$

   C. $3z$

   D. $\dfrac{z}{3}$

3. If Matthew earns three dollars per hour and $h$ is the number of hours that Matthew works, what expression represents how much money Matthew earns?

   A. $3 + h$

   B. $h - 3$

   C. $3h$

   D. $\dfrac{h}{3}$

## Solving Linear Equations

An equation is an expression that involves numbers, variables and an equal sign. When we solve equations, our goal is to get the variable by itself. In order to get the variable by itself, we do the inverse operation. For example, to eliminate addition, we use subtraction. To eliminate division, we use multiplication.

| Example 1 | Solve for $x$: $x - 5 = 16$ |

## Solution:

To get $x$ by itself, we must move the $-5$ to the other side of the equation. Thus, we add 5 to both sides of the equation to get $x$ by itself.

$$x - 5 = 16$$
$$x - 5 + 5 = 16 + 5$$
$$x = 21$$

| Example 2 | Solve for $x$: $4x = 20$ |

## Solution:

To eliminate multiplication, we divide both sides of the equation by 4.

$$4x = 20$$
Thus   $$\frac{4x}{4} = \frac{20}{4}$$
$$x = 5$$

| Example 3 | Solve for $x$: $\frac{x}{3} = 1$ |

## Solution:

To eliminate division by 3, we multiply both sides of the equation by 3.
  Thus,

$$\frac{x}{3} = 11$$

$$3 \times \frac{x}{3} = 11 \times 3$$

$$x = 33$$

Equations can be used to model real-life situations.

**Example 4**    If Diana has 4 more dollars than Mary has, and Diana has 16 dollars, how many dollars does Mary have?

## Solution:

We let $d$ = the number of dollars that Mary has. Since Diana has 4 more dollars than Mary, we write $d + 4 = 16$, because Diana has 16 dollars. Now, we solve the equation.

$$d + 4 = 16$$
$$d + 4 - 4 = 16 - 4$$
$$d = 12$$

Thus, Mary has 12 dollars.

## Lesson Practice

In questions 1–4, solve the equation for $x$.

1.   $x + 11 = 21$  $X = 10$ ✓

2.   $3x = 36$  $X = 12$ ✓

3.   $\dfrac{x}{4} = 12$  $X = 48$ ✓

4.   $x - 14 = 2$  $X = 16$ ✓

In questions 5 and 6, write an equation that describes the situation and then solve the equation.

5.   Jason walks four blocks further to school than Michael walks. If Michael walks 6 blocks, how many blocks does Jason walk? Let $b$ = the number of blocks that Jason walks.  $b - 4 = 6$ ✗

6.   Cale's grade on the first test was 10 points higher than his grade on the second test. If his grade on the first test was 79, what was his grade on the second test? Let $x$ = Cale's grade on the second test.  $x + 10 = 79$ ✗

$$) + 4 = 6$$

## Test Preparation Practice

Circle the letter of the correct answer.

1.  For which equation is the solution $x = 4$?

    A.  $4x = 4$

    B.  $x - 4 = 4$

    C.  $x + 4 = 4$

    D.  $x + 4 = 8$

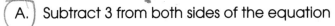

2.  How do you solve $x + 3 = 16$?

    A.  Subtract 3 from both sides of the equation

    B.  Add 3 to both sides of the equation

    C.  Divide both sides of the equation by 3

    D.  Multiply both sides of the equation by 3

3.  If Jeremy ate 6 cookies and Jennifer ate twice as many cookies as Jeremy did, which equation could be solved to find how many cookies Jennifer ate? Let $c$ = the number of cookies Jennifer ate.

    A.  $6 \times 2 = c$

    B.  $\dfrac{6}{2} = c$

    C.  $2c = 6$

    D.  $c + 2 = 6$

## Algebraic Sentences Involving Inequalities

Not all expressions have to be written with an equal sign. When an equal sign is used, we call the expression an equation. However, there are other symbols that can be used that are called inequalities. The most common inequalities are listed in the table below.

| Symbol | Description in Words |
|--------|---------------------|
| > | Is greater than |
| < | Is less than |
| ≥ | Is greater than or equal to |
| ≤ | Is less than or equal to |
| ≠ | Is not equal to |

The solution to an inequality is every number that makes the inequality true.

**Example 1**    **Give three possible solutions to the inequality $x \leq 4$.**

## Solution:

Since $x$ is less than or equal to 4, we must choose three values for $x$ that are less than or equal to 4. Thus, three possibilities are 4, 1, and 0.

**Example 2**    **Fill in the blank with either >, <, or =**

a)  4 _____ > _____ 3

b)  −5 _____ < _____ 1

c)  3 − 4 _____ < _____ 5 + 3

## Solutions:

a)   4 ___>___ 3

b)   −5 ___<___ 1

c)   3 − 4 _____ 5 + 3 is the same as −1 __<_ 8

Often, inequalities are used to describe real life situations. Words that indicate the need to use an inequality are "at least" and "at most."

**Example 3**    **Write an algebraic expression that represents the phrase, "Timmy has at least 30 dollars." Let *d* = the number of dollars that Timmy has.**

## Solution:

$d \geq 30$

 **Lesson Practice**

For questions 1–4, fill in the blank with >, <, or =.

1.   −6 _<_ −4

2.   $a + 3$ _>_ 7, if $a = 5$

3.   $(2 + 6)^2$ _>_ $4 \times (10 + 5)$

4.   64 % _<_ $5^2 + 6^2$

# Test Preparation Practice

Circle the letter of the correct answer.

1.  Which inequality represents the phrase "Jackie can spend at most 15 dollars."
    Let $d$ represent Jackie's dollars.

    A.   $d < 15$

    B.   $d > 15$

    C.   $d \leq 15$

    D.   $d \geq 15$

2.  Bernie needs at least an 80 on his next test to earn an A in the class. Which of
    the following grades would not earn Bernie an A?

    A.   100

    B.   90

    C.   80

    D.   70

3.  Which symbol makes the statement true?
    $$4 + 3 \times 3 \underline{\quad} 5 + 5 \times 2$$

    A.   $>$

    B.   $<$

    C.   $=$

    D.   $\geq$

4.  Suppose $x = 9$. Which of the following is false?

    A.   $x < 4^2$

    B.   $x > 3^2$

    C.   $x \geq 3^2$

    D.   $x \leq 3^2$

# Chapter 11—Solutions

## Evaluating Numerical and Algebraic Expressions

### Lesson Practice

1. 20
2. 10
3. 56
4. 7
5. $3j$
6. $J + 14$

### Test Preparation Practice

1. B
2. C
3. C

## Solving Linear Equations

### Lesson Practice

1. 10
2. 12
3. 48
4. 16
5. $b = 6 + 4$
6. $x = 79 - 10$

### Test Preparation Practice

1. D
2. A
3. A

## Algebraic Sentences Involving Inequalities

### Lesson Practice

1. $<$
2. $>$
3. $>$
4. $<$

### Test Preparation Practice

1. C
2. D
3. B
4. B

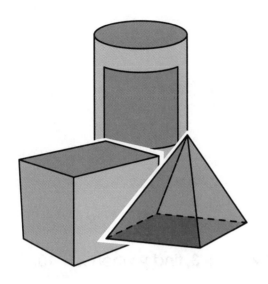

# Chapter 12
# Modeling

## Model Descriptions of Situations by Using Patterns, Relations, and Functions

A relation is some set of paired data, often displayed as a table of two values. This table can often be changed into an equation that shows the relationship. If one variable depends on another variable, we call the relation a function.

**Example 1**  Write an equation that describes *y* as a function of *x*.

| x | y |
|---|---|
| 1 | 5 |
| 2 | 10 |
| 3 | 15 |
| 4 | 20 |
| 5 | 25 |

## Solution:

In order to find an equation of *y* as a function of *x*, we must determine the pattern that relates *x* and *y*.

It appears that as *x* increases by 1, *y* increases by 5. We could write this pattern as follows:

$x = 1, y = 5$

$x = 2, y = 5 + 5 = 5 \times 2$

$x = 3, y = 5 + 5 + 5 = 5 \times 3$

$x = 4, y = 5 + 5 + 5 + 5 = 5 \times 4$

$x = 5, y = 5 + 5 + 5 + 5 + 5 = 5 \times 5$

So, we say that $y = 5$ times $x$.

Thus, the equation that describes $y$ as a function of $x$ is $y = 5x$.

**Example 2**    If $y$ is a function of $x$, and $y = x + 3$, find $y$ when $x = 10$.

## Solution:

We substitute 10 in for $x$. Thus, $y = 10 + 3 = 13$.

**Example 3**    Using $h$ to represent the number of hours of bike rental and $C$ to represent the cost of the bike rental, write an equation that describes the cost of renting a bike if the bike costs 10 dollars per hour plus a 5-dollar standard fee.

## Solution:

Because the bike costs 10 dollars per hour, we have to multiply 10 times the number of hours, $h$. Then, we have to add 5 dollars to our total cost. Thus, our equation is $C = 10h + 5$.

## Lesson Practice

For questions 1–2, evaluate the function at the indicated value.

1.  $y = 3x - 5$, $x = 4$    $y = 7$

2.  $C = \dfrac{r}{5} + 10$, $r = 30$    $C = 16$

3.  Write an equation that describes the following table of values:

| x | y |
|---|---|
| 5 | 7 |
| 6 | 8 |
| 7 | 9 |

_____ $x + 2 = y$ _____

## Test Preparation Practice

Circle the letter of the correct answer.

1.  Which equation describes the distance ($d$) that a car travels if a car drives for $h$ hours at 50 miles per hour?

    A.  $h = 50d$

    B.  $d = 50h$

    C.  $d = 50 + h$

    D.  $h = 50 + d$

2.  What number correctly fills in the next space in the table?

| 5 | 10 |
|---|----|
| 6 | 12 |
| 7 | 14 |
| 8 | ? |

A.  15

B.  16

C.  17

D.  18

3.  If $y = 10x + 14$, what does $y$ equal if $x = 6$?

A.  60

B.  66

C.  70

D.  74

4.  A cell phone plan charges a 25 dollar per month fee plus $0.01 dollars per minute of cell phone use. If $C$ equals the cost per month of the plan and $m$ equals the number of minutes a person uses the phone, which equation represents the cost of using the cell phone?

A.  $C = 0.01 + m$

B.  $C = 0.01m - 25$

C.  $C = 0.01m + 25$

D.  $C = 25m + 0.01$

### Drawing Graphs and Making Predictions About Events, Changes Over Time, and Relations Between Quantities

A common relation is the ordered pair. Ordered pairs are written in the form $(x, y)$ and are graphed on the $xy$-coordinate system.

**Example 1**    Graph the following ordered pairs on the axis below.
(2,2), (4,5), (6,4)

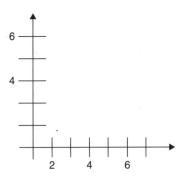

**Solution:**

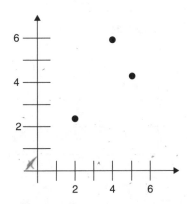

Graphs often relate two variables, the horizontal axis represents the independent variable and the vertical axis represents the dependent axis. We can make predictions based on graphs.

**Example 2**    Sketch a graph of what you would expect a graph relating a person's height and weight to look like. Graph the height on the horizontal axis and weight on the vertical axis.

## Solution:

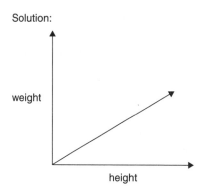

We would expect a person's weight to increase as a person's height increases.

Graphs are also made by following a functional rule. For example $y = x + 2$ is a functional rule that means for every number that is substituted into $x$, there is a $y$ value that is 2 units greater than the $x$ value. To graph functions given by rules, we make a table of values and then plot the order pairs. Finally, we connect the ordered pairs with a line.

**Example 3** **Fill in the table of values for the function $y = x + 3$, then graph the ordered pairs.**

| Functional Rule: $y = x + 3$ | | |
|---|---|---|
| **x-value** | **x + 3** | **y-value** |
| 1 | | |
| 2 | | |
| 3 | | |

## Solution:

| Functional Rule: $y = x + 3$ | | |
|---|---|---|
| **x-value** | **x + 3** | **y-value** |
| 1 | 1 + 3 | 4 |
| 2 | 2 + 3 | 5 |
| 3 | 3 + 3 | 6 |

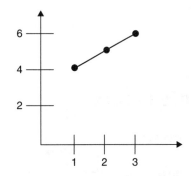

## Lesson Practice

1.  Fill in the table of values for the function $y = (x - 1) \times 2$, and then make a graph of the function.

| Functional Rule: $y = (x - 1) \times 2$ | | |
| --- | --- | --- |
| **x-value** | **(x − 1) × 2** | **y-value** |
| 1  1 | (1−1)×2 | 0 |
| 2 | (2−1)×2 | 2 |
| 3 | (3−1)×2 | 4 |

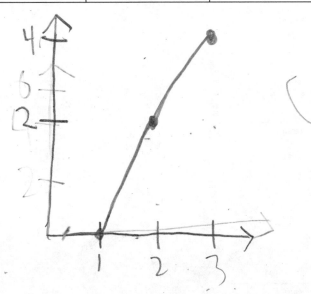

## Test Preparation Practice

Circle the letter of the correct answer.

1. Which graph below best represents the temperature during a 24-hour period in Fortescue, New Jersey, during the month of November?

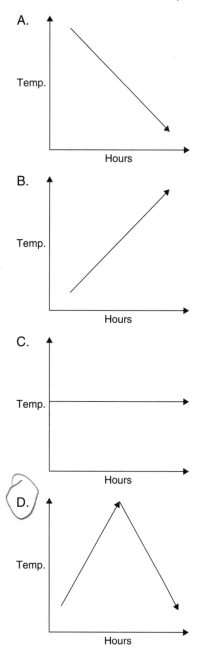

A.

Temp.

Hours

B.

Temp.

Hours

C.

Temp.

Hours

D.

Temp.

Hours

2.  What would you expect that a graph relating the amount of money earned and the number of hours worked would look like?

   A.  a horizontal line

   B.  a vertical line

   C.  a line that rises from left to right

   D.  a line that falls from left to right

3.  What would the $y$-value be if $y = \dfrac{x+2}{4}$, if $x = 10$?

   A.  4.5

   B.  2.5

   C.  3.5

   D.  3

 # Chapter 12—Solutions

## Model Descriptions of Situations by Using Patterns, Relations, and Functions

### Lesson Practice

1. 7
2. 16
3. $y = x + 2$

### Test Preparation Practice

1. B
2. B
3. D
4. C

## Drawing Graphs and Making Predictions About Events, Changes Over Time, and Relations Between Quantities

### Lesson Practice

1.

| Functional Rule: $y = (x - 1) \times 2$ | | |
|---|---|---|
| **x-value** | **$(x - 1) \times 2$** | **y-value** |
| 1 | $(1 - 1) \times 2$ | 0 |
| 2 | $(2 - 1) \times 2$ | 2 |
| 3 | $(3 - 1) \times 2$ | 4 |

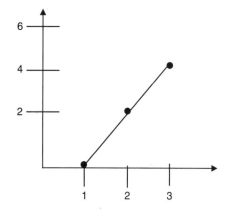

### Test Preparation Practice

1. D
2. C
3. D

# Unit IV

## Data Analysis, Probability, and Discrete Mathematics

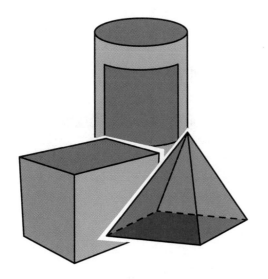

# Chapter 13
# Data Analysis

## Read and Interpret Graphs

Graphs can be used to display data and we can make predictions based on the graph. There are several common graphs that are used to display data. These include bar graphs, line graphs, and circle graphs.

A bar graph is used to compare data.

| **Example 1** | Using the bar graph below, answer the questions that follow. |

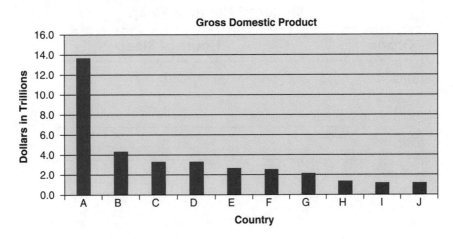

a) Which country had the largest GDP (Gross Domestic Product)?

_____

b) Which country had a smaller GDP, country F or country J?

_____

c) About how many times larger is country A's GDP than country B's GDP?

_____

## Solutions:

a) Country A has the largest GDP.

b) Country J has a smaller GDP than country F.

c) Since country A's GDP is slightly less than 14 trillion and country B's GDP is slightly larger than 4 trillion, country A's GDP is about 3 times as large as country B's GDP.

To make a bar graph, we follow a 3-step process.

Step 1: Choose a reasonable scale and interval. This means to pick reasonable numbers for the vertical axis.

Step 2: Label the horizontal and vertical axes and give the graph a title.

Step 3: Draw the vertical bars that represent the data.

| Example 2 | Draw a bar graph that represents the data in the table below. |

| Students' Hours of Sleep | |
|---|---|
| **Grade** | **Hours of Sleep** |
| 3rd | 7 |
| 5th | 8 |
| 7th | 8 |
| 10th | 5 |

## Solution:

Step 1: Since the data includes numbers from 5–8, a scale from 0 to 9 makes sense and an interval of one unit makes sense.

Step 2: Label the horizontal axis "Grade" and the vertical axis "Hours of Sleep." Give the graph the title "Students' Hours of Sleep."

Step 3: Draw the bars of each grade.

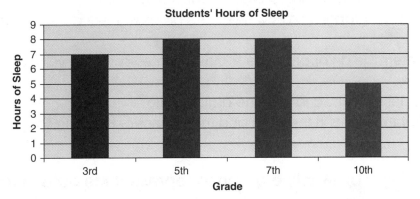

Line graphs are a way to show how data changes over time. When we make line graphs, the horizontal axis should always be labeled as some quantity of time.

| **Example 3** | **Using the line graph below, answer the questions that follow.** |

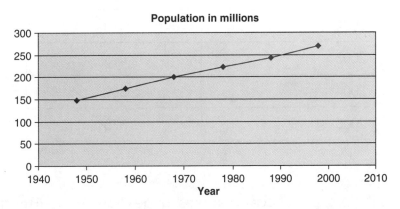

a)  What was the population in 1970? _____

b)  Will the population be greater or less than 300 million in 2010?

_____

c)  About how much did the population increase from 1950 to 1990?

_____

## Solutions:

a)  200 million

b)  Based on the trend, the population will be greater than 300 million in the year 2010.

c)  In 1950, the population was about 150 million. In 1990, the population was about 250 million. The increase is about 100 million.

To create a line graph, we follow the same process as we did to create the bar graph.

Step 1: Determine an appropriate scale and interval for the vertical and horizontal axes.

Step 2: Label the axes and give the graph a title.

Step 3: Plot the points in the data and then connect the data with lines.

**Example 4**    **Draw a line graph to represent the data in the table.**

| Car Accidents in Anytown, U.S.A. | |
|---|---|
| **Year** | **Number of Accidents** |
| 2000 | 359 |
| 2001 | 338 |
| 2002 | 410 |
| 2003 | 416 |
| 2004 | 389 |
| 2005 | 375 |

## Solution:

Step 1: Since the number of car accidents ranges from 338 to 416, an appropriate scale would be 300 to 440 and an appropriate interval will be 15.

Step 2: We label the horizontal axis "Years" and the vertical axis "Number of Accidents" and we title the graph "Car Accidents by Year in Anytown, U.S.A."

Step 3: Plot the points and connect the points with line segments.

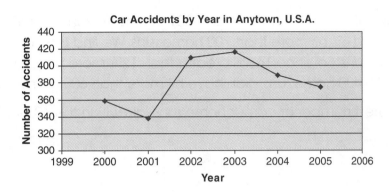

Car Accidents by Year in Anytown, U.S.A.

Circle graphs (also called pie charts) are used to compare parts to a whole. The parts of a circle graph are usually presented as percentages. So, the sum of all the parts of a circle graph must equal 100%.

**Example 5**  **Using the circle graph below, answer the questions that follow.**

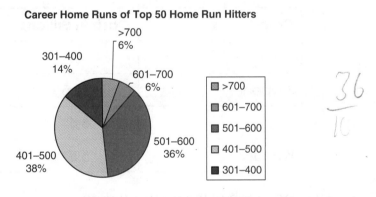

Career Home Runs of Top 50 Home Run Hitters

$\dfrac{36}{10}$

a)  Of the top 50 home run hitters, how many have hit between 501–600 home runs? ___36% (players)___ → (Technically 19, since Albert Pujols recently h

b)  Have more people hit between 301 and 400 home runs, or more than 600 home runs? ___More hit between 301 and 400.___

c)  According to the chart, what range contains the greatest number of career home runs? ___401-500 home runs___

## Solutions:

a)  To convert a percentage to the actual number, we must multiply the percentage by the total number of data in the chart. Since this chart represents 50 home run hitters, we multiply 50 × 36% = 50 × 0.36 = 18. There are 18 home run hitters who hit between 501–600 home runs.

b)  Since 14% of the hitters hit between 301–400 home runs and 6% hit between 601–700 and 6% hit more than 700 home runs. We find that 12% hit more than 600 home runs. So, since 14% is greater than 12%, more people have hit between 301–400 home runs than have hit more than 600 home runs.

c)  The greatest number of career home runs falls within the 401–500 range.

## Lesson Practice

1.  Construct a bar graph of the following data:

| Major Crops Grown | |
|---|---|
| **Crop** | **Cash in Billions** |
| Corn | 15.1 |
| Soybeans | 12.5 |
| Hay | 3.4 |
| Wheat | 5.5 |

2.  Construct a line graph of the following data:

| Amount of Money in Steve's Savings Account | |
|---|---|
| January | $25.00 |
| April | $90.00 |
| July | $175.00 |
| October | $142.00 |

## Test Preparation Practice

Circle the letter of the correct answer.
For questions 1–3, use the bar graph below.

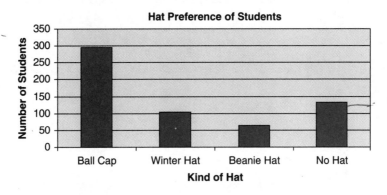

1.  About how many students prefer a winter hat?

    A.  300

    B.  200

    C.  100

    D.  50

2.  About how many more students prefer no hat to a beanie hat?

    A.  100

    B.  140

    C.  80

    D.  30

3.  About how many students were surveyed for this data?

    A.  200

    B.  400

    C.  600

    D.  800

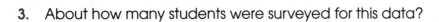

For questions 4–6, use the line graph below.

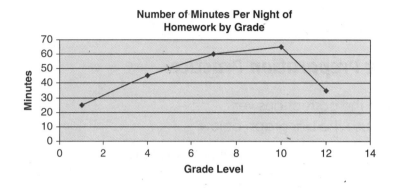

**Number of Minutes Per Night of Homework by Grade**

4. How many more minutes of homework does a 10th grader do every night than a 4th grader?

    A. 65 minutes

    B. 45 minutes

    C. 110 minutes

    D. 20 minutes

5. About how many minutes of homework does a 5th grader do each night?

    A. 30

    B. 40

    C. 50

    D. 60

6. According to the graph, what grade level does about the same amount of homework each night as 12th graders?

    A. 3rd grade

    B. 5th grade

    C. 9th grade

    D. 11th grade

For questions 7 and 8, use the circle graph below.

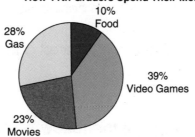

**How 11th Graders Spend Their Money**

10% Food

28% Gas

39% Video Games

23% Movies

7.  If 200 11th graders were surveyed, how many said they spend their money on gas?

    A.  56

    B.  28

    C.  78

    D.  20

8.  What percent of students spend their money on food?

    A.  10

    B.  23

    C.  28

    D.  39

## *Finding the Range, Median, and Mean*

When looking at data and statistics, we have certain numbers that are particularly useful. The range, median, and mean are statistical numbers that are very useful.

The range is the difference between the greatest and smallest values in a data set.

**Example 1**    **Find the range of the following set of numbers:**
**{12, 14, 19, 26, 27, 42}.**

## Solution:

Since the range is a difference, we subtract the smallest number from the largest number. Range = 42 − 12 = 30.

The mean is also called the average of a set of data. To find the mean, we add all of the numbers together and then divide by how many numbers are in the data.

**Example 2**    **Find the mean of the following set of numbers:**
**{12, 14, 19, 26, 27, 42}.**

## Solution:

Mean = (12 + 14 + 19 + 26 + 27 + 42) ÷ 6 = 140 ÷ 6 = 23.33.

The median is the middle number of a set of data. To find the median, we put the data in order from smallest to largest and then determine which number is in the middle. If there are two numbers in the middle, we find the mean of those two numbers.

**Example 3**    **Find the median of the following set of numbers:**
**{12, 14, 19, 26, 27, 42}.**

## Solution:

Since the data is already ordered from smallest to largest, we cross off numbers from both sides of the data until we meet in the middle.

~~12~~, ~~14~~, 19, 26, ~~27~~, ~~42~~.

Since there are two numbers in the middle, we find the mean of these two numbers:
(19 + 26) ÷ 2 = 45 ÷ 2 = 22.5

 **Lesson Practice**

For questions 1–3, use the following set of numbers:
{13, 45, 61, 22, 31}

1.  Find the range of the data. _____

2.  Find the mean of the data. _____

3.  Find the median of the data. _____

 **Test Preparation Practice**

Circle the letter of the correct answer.

1.  Find the median of 15, 26, 20, 33, 45, 11.

    A.  20

    B.  23

    C.  26

    D.  33

2.  Find the mean of 7, 9, 13, 26, 41.

    A.  13

    B.  17

    C.  20.5

    D.  19.2

3. Find the range of 14, 29, 68, 11, 38, 45.

   A. 38

   B. 45

   C. 57

   D. 34.2

# Chapter 13—Solutions

## Read and Interpret Graphs

### Lesson Practice

1.

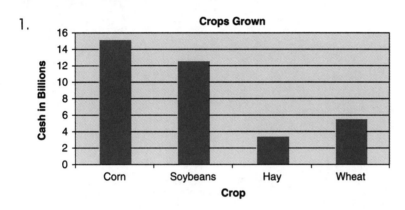

2.

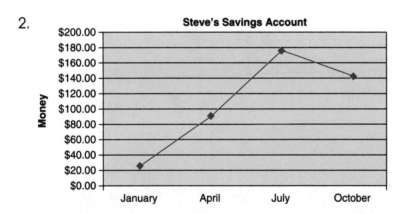

### Test Preparation Practice

1. C
2. C
3. C
4. D
5. C
6. A
7. B
8. A

Both Wrong

243

## *Finding the Range, Median, and Mean*

| **Lesson Practice** | **Test Preparation Practice** |
|---|---|
| 1. 48 | 1. B |
| 2. 34.4 | 2. D |
| 3. 31 | 3. C |

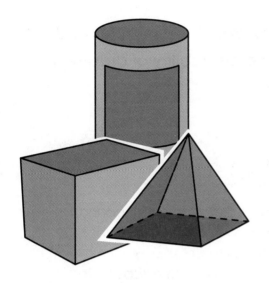

# Chapter 14
# Probability

## Finding the Probability of an Event and the Probability of the Complement of an Event

Probability is a ratio, often written as a fraction, that compares the possible number of desired outcomes of an event to the total number of outcomes of an event.

$$\text{We usually write } P(E) = \frac{\text{number of favorable outcomes of an event}}{\text{total number of possible outcomes of an event}}.$$

$P(E)$ stands for the "probability of an event." We consider "favorable outcomes" to be the outcomes that we are looking for. Although probabilities are usually written as fractions, they can also be converted to decimals or percentages.

**Example 1**   **In a deck of cards, there are 15 green cards, 15 red cards, 15 black cards, and 15 blue cards. If a card is drawn at random from the deck of cards, what is the probability that the card is red?**

### Solution:

$$\text{The probability of a red card} = \frac{\text{number of red cards}}{\text{total number of cards}} = \frac{15}{60} = \frac{1}{4}.$$

**Example 2**    If a bag of 15 marbles contains 6 red marbles and 9 blue marbles, what is the probability of drawing a blue marble at random?

## Solution:

$$P(blue\ marble) = \frac{\text{number of blue marbles}}{\text{total number of marbles}} = \frac{9}{15} = \frac{3}{5}.$$

When writing probabilities, a probability of 0 means that an event cannot happen. A probability of 1 means that an event has to happen. The closer a probability is to 1, the more likely an event is to occur.

When we wish to find the probability that an event does not happen, we are trying to find the probability of the complement. To find the probability of a complement, we subtract the probability of an event from 1.

**Example 3**    A deck of cards contains 5 red cards, 12 blue cards, 15 black cards, and 8 green cards. What is the probability of NOT drawing a black card?

## Solution:

Not drawing a black card is the complement of drawing a black card. So, the

probability of not drawing a black card = $1 - P(Black\ Card) = 1 - \frac{15}{40} = \frac{25}{40} = \frac{5}{8}.$

**Example 4**    A deck of cards contains 5 red cards, 12 blue cards, 15 black cards, and 8 green cards. What is the probability of drawing a purple card?

## Solution:

Since there are no purple cards, this is an impossible event. So, the probability of drawing a purple card is 0.

## Lesson Practice

For questions 1–4, use the following information:
A bowl of potato chips contains 35 regular chips, 45 salt and vinegar chips, 25 sour cream and onion chips, and 25 barbecue chips.

1.  Find the probability of drawing a barbecue chip at random. $\frac{5}{26}$ ✓

2.  Find the probability of not drawing a regular chip at random. $\frac{7}{26}$ ✗

3.  What is the probability of drawing a pizza-flavored chip from the bag?
    0 ✓

4.  Find the probability of NOT drawing a salt and vinegar chip. $\frac{17}{26}$ ✓

## Test Preparation Practice

Circle the letter of the correct answer.

Questions 1–4 all refer to the following situation:
A bag of marbles contains 6 red marbles, 7 green marbles, 2 black marbles, and 5 blue marbles.

1.  What is the probability of drawing a red marble?

    A. $\frac{3}{10}$

    B.  0.4

    C.  0.6

    D. $\frac{7}{10}$

2.  What is the probability of NOT drawing a black marble?

    A.  0.1

    B.  0.9

    C.  0

    D.  1

3.  What is the probability of drawing a green marble?

    A.  0.6

    B.  0.35

    C.  1

    D.  0.4

4.  What is the probability of drawing a blue marble?

    A.  75%

    B.  25%

    C.  35%

    D.  65%

## Using the Multiplication Rule for Probabilities and Determining Probabilities from Experiments

When we want to find the probability that two events will both occur, we multiply the probability that the first event occurs and the probability that the second event occurs.

**Example 1**    On a fair six-sided number cube, the numbers 1–6 are all equally likely to appear. What is the probability that if a six-sided number cube is rolled twice, both times a 6 comes up on the number cube?

## Solution:

Since there are two events, we must multiply the probability of each event.

$$P(6,6) = P(6) \times P(6) = \frac{1}{6} \times \frac{1}{6} = \frac{1}{36}.$$

**Example 2**    **If the probability of getting an A in English class is 0.3 and the probability of getting an A in German class is 40%, what is the possibility that a student gets an A in both English and German?**

## Solution:

We need to multiply the two probabilities. First, we should convert 40% to a decimal. 40% = 0.4. Now, we multiply the two probabilities. *P(E)* = (0.3) × (0.4) = 0.12.

We often use experiments to predict the probability of an event occurring. Experimental probability is found by dividing the number of times of event occurs by the total number of experimental trials.

**Example 3**    **Anna performed an experiment in which she counted the number of cars that either ran a stop sign, came to a complete stop, or rolled through the stop sign. Her data is displayed below:**

| Total Cars | Complete Stop | Rolling Stop | Ran the Stop Sign |
|---|---|---|---|
| 215 | 65 | 120 | 30 |

a)  What is the probability that a car will come to a complete stop at the stop sign? _____

b)  What is the probability that a car will NOT come to a complete stop at the stop sign? _____

c)  What is the probability that two consecutive cars will each make a rolling stop? _____

## Solutions:

a)   The probability that the car will come to a complete stop =

$$\frac{\text{number of complete stops}}{\text{number of cars}} = \frac{65}{215} = \frac{13}{43}$$

b)   The probability that the car will not come to a complete stop =

$$1 - \text{probability that the car comes to a complete stop} = 1 - \frac{13}{43} = \frac{30}{43}.$$

c)   The probability that two consecutive cars make a rolling stop at the stop sign is equal to the probability of the first car making a rolling stop times the probability of the second car making a rolling stop.

$$P(E) = P(\text{Rolling Stop}) \times P(\text{Rolling Stop}) = \frac{120}{215} \times \frac{120}{215} = 0.56 \times 0.56 = 0.31$$

## Lesson Practice

For questions 1–4, use the experimental data below.

A company tests to see how many of its computers are defective. The data is displayed in the table below.

| Number Tested | Good Condition | Defective Condition |
|---|---|---|
| 8,000 | 7,408 | 592 |

1.   What percentage of the computers were found to be defective?

_____7.4%_____

2.   What is the probability that a computer chosen at random will be in good condition? _____

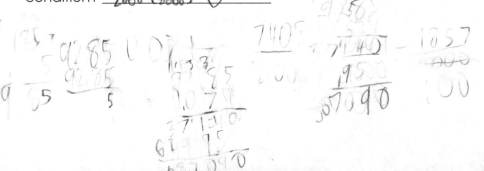

3. If two computers are chosen at random, what is the probability that the first computer will be in good condition and the second computer will be defective? __0.068709 ✓__

4. If three computers are chosen at random, what is the probability that all three will be in good condition? __0.8005 ✓__ (as long as work is shown)

## Test Preparation Practice

Circle the letter of the correct answer.

Use the data in the table below to answer questions 1–3.
A person keeps track of the color of cars that come up for bid at an auction. The data is displayed in the table.

| Total Number of Cars Observed = 450 | |
| --- | --- |
| Color of Car | Number of Cars of the Color |
| Red | 172 |
| Black | 120 |
| Navy Blue | 31 |
| Yellow | 127 |

1. What is the probability that the next car up for bid at the auction is yellow?

   A. 38%

   B. 27%

   C. 0.2%

   D. 28%

2. What is the probability that the next car is NOT red?

A. 0.38

B. 0.27

C. 0.62

D. 0.72

3. If the person conducting the experiment tracked 2000 cars, about how many would you expect to be navy blue?

A. 120

B. 140

C. 160

D. 180

4. If an experiment shows that the probability that a television will burn out in the next three years is $\frac{1}{15}$ and 4,000 televisions were tested in the experiment, about how many televisions burned out within three years?

A. 100

B. 260

C. 450

D. 900

 # Chapter 14—Solutions

## Finding the Probability of an Event and the Probability of the Complement of an Event

**Lesson Practice**

1. $\dfrac{25}{130}$

2. $\dfrac{95}{130}$

3. 0

4. $\dfrac{85}{130}$

**Test Preparation Practice**

1. A
2. B
3. B
4. B

## Using the Multiplication Rule for Probabilities and Determining Probabilities from Experiments

**Lesson Practice**

1. 7.4%
2. 0.926
3. $(0.926) \times (0.074) = 0.069$
4. $(0.926) \times (0.926) \times (0.926) = 0.794$

**Test Preparation Practice**

1. D
2. C
3. B
4. B

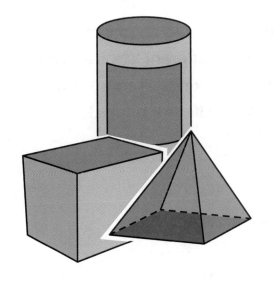

# Chapter 15
## Discrete Mathematics— Counting

## Solving Counting Problems

When we want to find how many different ways a group of objects can be ordered, we count arrangements. To count arrangements, we multiply all the different ways that are possible.

**Example 1**   There are 25 runners in a race. How many different ways can 1st, 2nd, and 3rd place prizes be awarded?

## Solution:

To find the total number of arrangements of 1st, 2nd, and 3rd places, we multiply the number of ways 1st place can be awarded, times the number of ways 2nd place can be awarded, times the number of ways 3rd place can be awarded.

$$\underset{\substack{\text{Number of} \\ \text{runners for} \\ \text{1st Place}}}{\underline{\hphantom{xxxx}}} \times \underset{\substack{\text{Number of} \\ \text{runners for} \\ \text{2nd Place}}}{\underline{\hphantom{xxxx}}} \times \underset{\substack{\text{Number of} \\ \text{runners for} \\ \text{3rd Place}}}{\underline{\hphantom{xxxx}}} = 25 \times 24 \times 23 = 13,800.$$

| Example 2 | For lunch, a student can choose one sandwich, one fruit and one drink. How many different lunches can be made if there are 4 different kinds of sandwiches, 3 different kinds of fruit, and 3 different drinks to choose from? |

## Solution:

We multiply the different possibilities for each food/drink group.

$$\underline{\text{Number of possible sandwiches}} \times \underline{\text{Number of possible fruits}} \times \underline{\text{Number of possible drinks}} = 4 \times 3 \times 3 = 36$$

A second way to count arrangements is to draw a tree diagram. The branches of the tree diagram show the possible arrangements.

| Example 3 | If a sandwich cart contains the following choices, how many sandwiches are possible? |

| Breads | Meats |
|--------|-------|
| White  | Ham   |
| Wheat  | Turkey |
| Rye    |       |

## Solution:

We construct a tree diagram as follows:

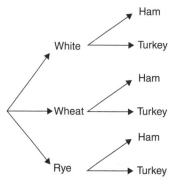

Now, we count the number of final branches. There are 6. So, there are 6 possible sandwiches.

Finally, we can use Venn diagrams to count how many objects appear in multiple sets. Venn diagrams are pictorial representations of sets.

**Example 4**    **How many numbers between 1 and 30 are divisible by both 2 and 3?**

## Solution:

We draw a Venn diagram.

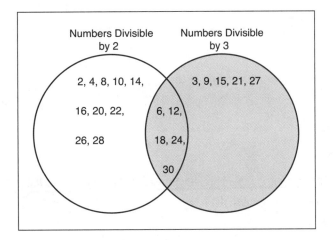

The numbers that appear in both sets are 6, 12, 18, 24, and 30.

## Lesson Practice

1.  If 6 people are going to choose 2 people to sit in the front seat of a car, with one in the driver's seat and one person in the passenger seat, how many different arrangements of people are possible to sit in the driver's seat and passenger's seat? ____30____ ✓

2.  How many different ways can a valet park 6 luxury cars in 6 parking spaces in a restaurant parking lot? ____720____ ✓

3.  Using a tree diagram, how many different outfits are possible if a person has 2 pairs of pants and 3 shirts to choose from? _____6_____

4.  Draw a Venn diagram to find how many numbers between 1 and 40 are divisible by both 5 and 10. _____4_____

## Test Preparation Practice

Circle the letter of the correct answer.

1.  If a coin is flipped three times, how many different outcomes are possible?

    A.  2

    B.  4

    C.  6

    D.  8

2.  If a 10-sided number cube is rolled and then a coin is flipped, how many different outcomes are possible?

    A.  10

    B.  2

    C.  12

    D.  20

3.  When picking a salad, Dave is given the choice of either a tossed salad, a Caesar salad, or a Cobb salad, and then must choose one of four possible dressings. How many different salad and dressing combinations are possible?

    A.  7

    B.  12

    C.  19

    D.  4

For questions 4–6, use the Venn diagram below.

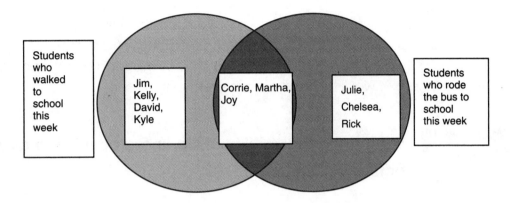

Students who walked to school this week

Jim, Kelly, David, Kyle

Corrie, Martha, Joy

Julie, Chelsea, Rick

Students who rode the bus to school this week

4.  How many students walked to school and rode the bus sometime during the past school week?

    A.  4

    B.  3

    C.  7

    D.  10

5.  Which of the following students only rode the bus to school this week?

    A.  Corrie

    B.  Jim

    C.  Kelly

    D.  Julie

6.  How many students only walked to school last week?

    A.  2

    B.  3

    C.  4

    D.  7

## Using the Multiplication Counting Principle

When we want to find the probability of several events happening, we are finding the probability of a compound event. To find the probability of a compound event, we find the ratio of the number of favorable ways the compound event can occur and the total number of ways the compound event can occur.

**Example 1**  What is the probability of flipping a coin twice and getting two heads (H-H)?

## Solution:

This is a compound event of flipping a coin twice. So, we have to count how many ways we can get H-H and how many total outcomes are possible for flipping a coin twice. In this case, we can just list the possible outcomes.

H-H, H-T, T-H, T-T

Since there is one way that H-H occurs and there are 4 possible outcomes, the probability of H-H = $\frac{1}{4}$.

Writing out the sample space only makes sense when there only a few possible outcomes. When solving problems with many outcomes, we have to multiply.

**Example 2**  If a person chooses one letter from the 26-letter alphabet and then rolls a 10-sided number cube, what is the probability that the person chooses the letter "E" and then rolls a 6?

## Solution:

To determine the total number of outcomes we have to determine how many ways any letter can be chosen and multiply that number by the number of ways that a 10-sided number cube can be rolled. Thus, the total number of possible outcomes = 26 × 10 = 260.

Now, we must determine how many ways an "E" and a 6 can be rolled. There is one way to choose an "E" and there is one way to roll a 6. Thus, the total number of ways to choose an "E" and roll a 6 = 1 × 1 = 1.

So, the probability of picking an "E" and then rolling a 6 = $\frac{1}{260}$.

$\dfrac{4}{8}$  ½

## Lesson Practice

For questions 1–2, use the following information.

8 cards are placed in a hat. On each card is one of the following letters: A, C, E, G, I, K, M, O. After a card is drawn, it is put back into the hat and a second card is drawn.

1.  What is the probability of drawing a vowel and then another vowel?

    $\dfrac{1}{4}$ ✓

2.  What is the probability of drawing a consonant and then a vowel?

    $\dfrac{1}{4}$ ✓

3.  If a coin is flipped three times, what is the probability of not flipping three tails (T-T-T)?  $\dfrac{7}{8}$ ✓

    $\dfrac{1}{2} \cdot \dfrac{1}{2} \cdot \dfrac{1}{2} = \dfrac{1}{8}$

## Test Preparation Practice

Circle the letter of the correct answer
Questions 1 and 2 refer to the spinners below.

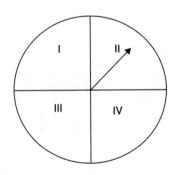

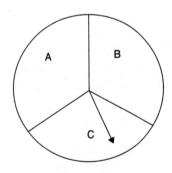

1.  What is the probability of spinning a II and then an A?

    A.  0.25

    B.  0.33

    C.  $\dfrac{1}{12}$ ✓

    D.  50%

2.  What is the probability of NOT spinning a III and then spinning a B?

    A.  0.25

    B.  0.33

    C.  $\frac{1}{12}$

    D.  50%

3.  If a 6-sided number cube is rolled twice, what is the probability of rolling an even number and then a 3?

    A.  0.25

    B.  0.33

    C.  $\frac{1}{12}$

    D.  50%

4.  If a bag contains a total of 15 marbles, and 3 marbles are red, 10 marbles are black, and 2 marbles are green, and we draw one marble, replace it, and then draw a second marble, what is the probability of drawing a red marble and then a black marble?

    A.  $\frac{3}{5}$

    B.  $\frac{2}{5}$

    C.  $\frac{2}{15}$

    D.  $\frac{3}{15}$

# Chapter 15—Solutions

## Solving Counting Problems

### Lesson Practice

1. $6 \times 5 = 30$
2. $6 \times 5 \times 4 \times 3 \times 2 \times 1 = 720$
3. 6
4.

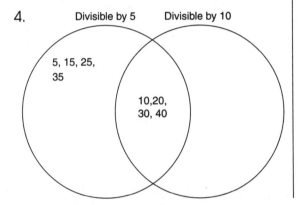

Divisible by 5     Divisible by 10

5, 15, 25, 35

10, 20, 30, 40

### Test Preparation Practice

1. D
2. D
3. B
4. B
5. D
6. C

## Using the Multiplication Counting Principle

### Lesson Practice

1. $\dfrac{1}{4}$
2. $\dfrac{1}{4}$
3. $\dfrac{7}{8}$

### Test Preparation Practice

1. C
2. A
3. C
4. C

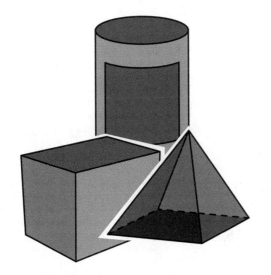

# Chapter 16
# Vertex Edge
# Graphs
# and Algorithms

## Developing Winning Strategies for Simple Games and Tasks

We can use simple processes to solve puzzles and win games. A common example is the magic square. In a magic square, the sum of the digits in each column, row, and diagonal is the same number and we only use each number once. The sum of each row, column, and diagonal is called the magic sum.

| Example 1 | Answer the following questions regarding the magic square: |

| 2 | 7 | ? |
|---|---|---|
| 9 | ? | ? |
| 4 | 3 | ? |

a) What is the sum of the columns? _____

b) What number must go in the top, right corner of the square? _____

c) What number must go in the middle square? _____

## Solutions:

a) The sum of the first column is 2 + 9 + 4 = 15

b) Since the sum of the rows and columns must be the same, the top row must add up to 15, since 2 + 7 = 9, the third number must be 15 − 9 = 6.

c) Since the sum of the middle column must be 15, and 7 + 3 = 10, the third number must be 5.

## Lesson Practice

1. Fill in the missing numbers in the magic square below.

| 6 | 1 | ? |
|---|---|---|
| ? | 5 | ? |
| ? | ? | 4 |

## Test Preparation Practice

Circle the letter of the correct answer.
For questions 1–4, use the magic square below.

| | | |
|---|---|---|
| 4 | 3 | 8 |
| ? | ? | 1 |
| 2 | ? | ? |

1. Which of the following is the sum of the diagonals?

    A.  4

    B.  12

    C.  15

    D.  20

2. What number must go in the center square?

    A.  5

    B.  6

    C.  7

    D.  9

3. What is the sum of all the numbers in the Magic Square?

   A. 9

   B. 15

   C. 30

   D. 45

4. What is the first step in finding a missing number in a magic square?

   A. Find the magic sum.

   B. Find possible missing numbers.

   C. Add up the other numbers in the same column.

   D. Add up the other numbers in the same row.

## Using Vertex Edge Graphs

A vertex edge graph is a system of points connected by line segments. The line segments are called edges and each point is called a vertex. Vertex edge graphs are often used to represent maps and to solve problems involving real-life situations.

**Example 1** Refer to the vertex edge graph below that shows Jim's part of town.

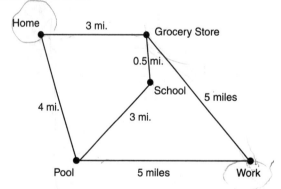

a) What is the shortest distance that Jim can drive to go from his house to work? _____

b) If Jim drives from home to work and then picks his child up after school and then returns home, how far did he drive? _____

c) Which is closer to home, the grocery store or the pool? _____

## Solutions:

a)   The shortest distance Jim can drive from home to work is 3 miles to the grocery store and then 5 miles to work. So, the total distance is 3 + 5 = 8 miles.

b)   The total distance will be the sum of each part of the trip. So, home to work = 8 miles, work to school = 5 + 0.5 = 5.5 miles, and school to home = 0.5 + 3 = 3.5 miles. So, the whole trip = 8 + 5.5 + 3.5 = 17 miles.

c)   Since the grocery store is 3 miles from home and the pool is 4 miles from home, the grocery store is closer to home than the pool.

In a vertex edge graph, two vertices that share a common edge are called neighboring vertices. A path on a vertex edge graph that begins and ends in the same place is called a circuit.

**Example 2**    **Consider the following vertex edge graph.**

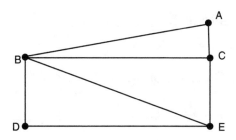

a)   How many vertices are there? _____

b)   Which vertices neighbor vertex D? _____

c)   How many edges are there? _____

## Solutions:

a)   There are 5 vertices – A, B, C, D, E.

b)   Vertex B and Vertex E neighbor vertex D.

c)   There are 7 edges.

## Lesson Practice

Questions 1–4 refer to the vertex edge graph below.

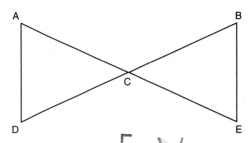

1. How many vertices are there? _____5_____ ✓

2. How many edges are there? _____6_____ ✓

3. Which vertices neighbor vertex A? _D, C_ ✓

4. Would the path A-D-C-A be considered a circuit? _Yes_ ✓

## Test Preparation Practice

Circle the letter of the correct answer.
Questions 1–4 refer to the vertex edge diagram below.

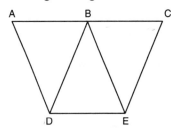

1. Which path below represents a circuit?

    A.  A-B-C

    B.  B-C-D

    C.  D-B-E-D

    D.  D-E-C-B

2.  How many vertices are there?

    A.  3

    B.  4

    C.  5

    D.  6

3.  How many edges are there?

    A.  5

    B.  7

    C.  9

    D.  10

4.  How many vertices neighbor B?

    A.  1

    B.  2

    C.  3

    D.  4

Questions 5–8 refer to the vertex edge graph below.

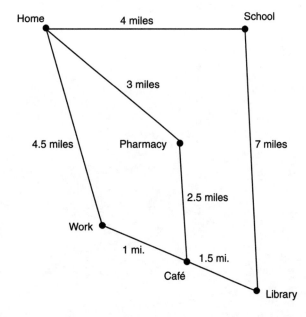

**5.** How far is the shortest distance from home to the library?

    A. 11 miles

    B. 8 miles

    C. 7 miles

    D. 6 miles

**6.** What is the shortest distance from school to work?

    A. 8 miles

    B. 8.5 miles

    C. 9 miles

    D. 9.5 miles

**7.** How many miles would a circuit from home to pharmacy to café to work back to home be?

    A. 8.5 miles

    B. 9.5 miles

    C. 11 miles

    D. 11.5 miles

**8.** What is the shortest distance from the café to the school?

    A. 8.5 miles

    B. 9 miles

    C. 9.5 miles

    D. 10 miles

 # Chapter 16—Solutions

## Developing Winning Strategies for Simple Games and Tasks

### Lesson Practice

1.

| 6 | 1 | 8 |
|---|---|---|
| 7 | 5 | 3 |
| 2 | 9 | 4 |

### Test Preparation Practice

1. C
2. A
3. D
4. A

## Using Vertex Edge Graphs

### Lesson Practice

1. 5
2. 6
3. C and D
4. Yes

### Test Preparation Practice

1. C
2. C
3. B
4. D
5. C
6. B
7. C
8. A

# Mathematics

This test is also on CD-ROM in our special interactive NJ ASK6 Mathematics TestWare®. It is highly recommended that you first take this exam on computer. You will then have the additional study features and benefits of enforced timed conditions and instant, accurate scoring.

## Directions to the Student

*The New Jersey Assessment of Skills and Knowledge (ASK) is a test of how well you understand mathematics. The test consists of two different types of questions: multiple-choice and open-ended.*

## There are several important things to remember:

**1** Read each question carefully and think about the answer. Then choose or write the answer that you think is best.

**2** When you are asked to select the answer, make sure you circle the letter of the correct answer.

**3** When you are asked to write your answers, write them neatly and clearly on the lines or in the space provided.

**4** If you finish a part of the test early, you may check over your work in that part.

**5** If you do not know the answer to a question, skip it and go on. You may return to it later if you have time.

**GO ON**

# MATHEMATICS REFERENCE SHEET

The sum of the measures of the interior angles of a triangle = 180°

Distance = rate × time

Simple Interest Formula: $A = p + prt$

A = amount after t years;  p = principal;  r = annual interest rate;  t = number of years

---

$\pi = 3.14$ or $\frac{22}{7}$

**Square**
Area = $s^2$
Perimeter = $4s$

**Rectangle**
Area = $lw$
Perimeter = $2l + 2w$

**Circle**
Area = $\pi r^2$
Circumference = $2\pi r$
  = $\pi d$

**Triangle**
Area = $\frac{1}{2} bh$

**Parallelogram**
Area = $bh$

**Trapezoid**
Area = $\frac{1}{2} h(b_1 + b_2)$

**Rectangular Prism**
Volume = $lwh$
Surface Area =
$2lw + 2wh + 2lh$

**Cylinder**
Volume = $\pi r^2 h$
Surface Area =
$2\pi rh + 2\pi r^2$

---

## USE THE FOLLOWING EQUIVALENTS FOR YOUR CALCULATIONS

| | | |
|---|---|---|
| 60 seconds = 1 minute | 12 inches = 1 foot | 10 millimeters = 1 centimeter |
| 60 minutes = 1 hour | 3 feet = 1 yard | 100 centimeters = 1 meter |
| 24 hours = 1 day | 36 inches = 1 yard | 10 decimeters = 1 meter |
| 7 days = 1 week | 5,280 feet = 1 mile | 1000 meters = 1 kilometer |
| 12 months = 1 year | 1,760 yards = 1 mile | |
| 365 days = 1 year | | |

| | |
|---|---|
| 8 fluid ounces = 1 cup | 16 ounces = 1 pound |
| 2 cups = 1 pint | 2,000 pounds = 1 ton |
| 2 pints = 1 quart | |
| 4 quarts = 1 gallon | 1000 milligrams = 1 gram |
| | 100 centigrams = 1 gram |
| 1000 milliliters (mL) = 1 liter (L) | 10 grams = 1 dekagram |
| | 1000 grams = 1 kilogram |

**GO ON**

**(Answer Sheets and a Mathematics Manipulative Sheet appear at the back of this book.)**

# Day 1

# Part I    Short Constructed-Response Questions

**Directions:** Solve each problem and write your answer on the answer sheet.
No calculator is permitted on this portion of the test.

1 Find the volume of the following figure in terms of $\pi$.

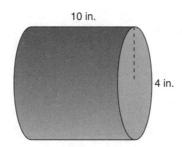

10 in.

4 in.

$160\,\pi$ ✓

2 How many edges does the following three-dimensional figure have?

9 edges ✓

**GO ON**

**3** If there are 5 red marbles, 4 green marbles, and 2 black marbles in a bag, what is the probability of randomly drawing one black marble?

$\dfrac{2}{11}$

**4** What is the perimeter of the parallelogram pictured below?

8 ft.

5 ft.

26 ft.

**5** Estimate 448.6 ÷ 49.2.

9

**6** Evaluate: 3 − (1 + 2) × 6.

−15

3 − 18

6/6

**GO ON**

280

# Part II  Multiple-Choice Questions

**Directions:** Fill in the correct choice on the answer sheet. Calculators are permitted for this portion of the test.

7 The Blue Jays junior high football team gained 35 yards after a loss of 6 yards on the previous play. On the third play, they lost 3 more yards. What is the Blue Jays' net yardage for the three plays?

A.  +26 yards

B.  +44 yards

C.  +32 yards

D.  −44 yards

8 Find the value of $x$ that makes $x - (-8) = 9$ a true sentence.

A.  1

B.  17

C.  −1

D.  −17

9 Which rule can be used to find the next number in the sequence below?

4, 8, 16, 32, ___

A.  Divide by 2

B.  Multiply by 2

C.  Subtract (−4)

D.  Add 16

10 Jamie has 6.75 cups of sugar. She is making a cake using a recipe that calls for 3.175 cups of sugar.  How much sugar will she have left?

A.  −9.925 cups

B.  −3.575 cups

C.  3.575 cups

D.  9.925 cups

**GO ON**

**11** Which of the following has a sum greater than 3?

A. $\frac{1}{2} + 1\frac{1}{2}$

B. $\frac{3}{4} + \frac{3}{4}$

C. $\frac{2}{3} + 2\frac{2}{3}$

D. $\frac{4}{3} + 1\frac{1}{3}$

**12** Joseph paid $3.55 for 40 sticks of bubble gum. What was the average price of each piece of bubble gum rounded to the nearest cent?

A. $0.11

B. $0.12

C. $0.08

D. $0.09

**13** Mrs. Johnson graded the English test for her fifth-grade class. The range of scores is 41. If the lowest grade is a 58, what is the highest grade?

A. 17

B. 58

C. 89

D. 99

**14** If the sum of two angles of a triangle measures 120 degrees, what does the third angle measure?

A. 240

B. 90

C. 60

D. 30

**15** How many lines of symmetry does a regular pentagon have?

A. 5

B. 6

C. 8

D. 0

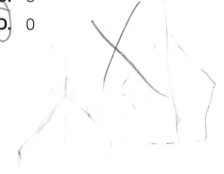

**GO ON**

**16** How many ice cream cone combinations are possible if you can choose chocolate or vanilla ice cream and a sugar cone or a waffle cone?

   **A.** 2

   **B.** 3

   **C.** 4

   **D.** 6

**17** What is the area of a triangle with a base of 4 inches and a height of 6 inches?

   **A.** 10 square inches

   **B.** 12 square inches

   **C.** 24 square inches

   **D.** 30 square inches

**18** What object could hold about 20 gallons of a liquid?

   **A.** Dinner glass

   **B.** Milk Jug

   **C.** Flower pot

   **D.** Bathtub

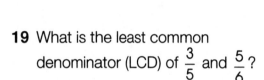

**19** What is the least common denominator (LCD) of $\frac{3}{5}$ and $\frac{5}{6}$?

   **A.** 5

   **B.** 6

   **C.** 11

   **D.** 30

**GO ON**

**20** Which object resembles a
rectangular prism?

   **A.** Tent

   **B.** Soda Can

   **C.** Box

   **D.** Candle

**21** Which weighs the least?

   **A.** 100 lbs.

   **B.** 0.25 tons

   **C.** 2,000 lbs.

   **D.** 2,000,000 oz.

**GO ON**

# Part III  Extended Constructed-Response Question

**Directions:** Write your answer neatly and clearly on the lines or in the space provided. Make sure to answer all of the parts of each question. The use of a calculator is permitted on this portion of the test.

**22** Use the vertex-edge graph below to answer the questions that follow.

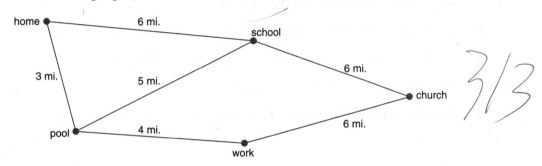

**a)** What is the shortest distance from home to work?

The shortest distance from home to work would be to pass the pool on the 3 mi. route and then go on the 4 mi. route to work. The distance would be 3 mi. + 4 mi. = 7 miles (shortest distance from home to work.)

**b)** How long would a round-trip from home to school to pool back to home be?

6 mi. + 5 mi. + 3 mi. = 14 mi.
(home to school)   (school to pool)  (pool to home)   The round-trip would be 14 miles.

**c)** Which is longer, a trip from work to school or from church to pool?

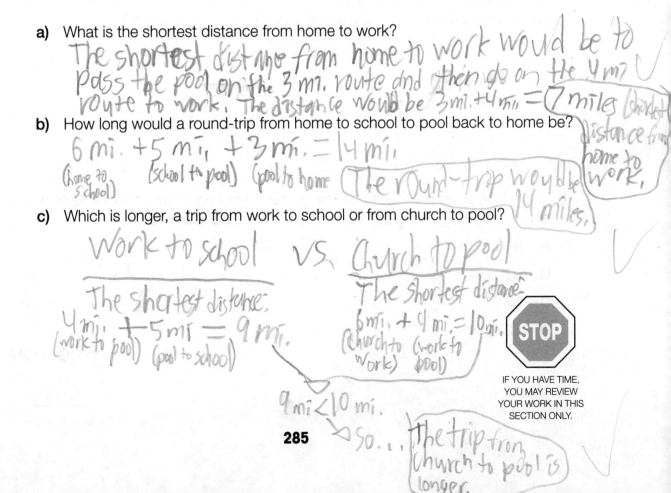

Work to school   vs.  Church to pool

The shortest distance:
4 mi. + 5 mi = 9 mi.
(work to pool) (pool to school)

The shortest distance:
6 mi. + 4 mi. = 10 mi.
(church to (work to
work)     pool)

9 mi < 10 mi.

So... The trip from church to pool is longer.

**STOP**

IF YOU HAVE TIME, YOU MAY REVIEW YOUR WORK IN THIS SECTION ONLY.

# Day 2

# Part I   Multiple-Choice Questions

**Directions:** Fill in the correct choice on the answer sheet. Calculators are

permitted for this portion of the test.

**1** Which of these must be measured precisely?

   **A.** The amount of time it takes to shower.

   **B.** The temperature during the day in January in New Jersey.

   **C.** The width of a cut to be made by a surgeon.

   **D.** The amount of time it takes to drive to school in the morning.

**2** At a go-kart track, 5 laps costs fifty cents. David has $4.50.  Which number sentence could you use to show how many laps David can buy?

   **A.** $9 + 5$

   **B.** $9 - 5$

   **C.** $9 \times 5$

   **D.** $9 \div 5$

**3** Jason built an engine in his technology class. His engine was sold for $234.91. If he spent $65.71 on parts for his engine, what was Jason's profit?

   **A.** $169.20

   **B.** $300.62

   **C.** $3.57

   **D.** $234.91

**GO ON**

**4** Solve the following equation for $x$.

$$x - 39 = 147$$

A. 5,733

B. 3.77

C. 108

D. 186

**5** If $z = 6$ and $y = 20$, what is the value of $y - 3z$?

A. 2

B. −54

C. 66

D. 38

**6** An elementary school auditorium has 600 seats in 25 equal rows. How many seats are in each row?

A. 10

B. 15

C. 20

D. 24

**7** Which decimal is equivalent to $\frac{7}{8}$?

A. 0.5

B. 1.875

C. 1.5

D. 0.875

**8** Maggie, James, Heath, and Sylvia are all running for classroom representative. Two students will be selected. How many different pairs of students can be selected?

A. 2

B. 3

C. 4

D. 6

**GO ON**

**9** Find the exact value of the expression below.

$$3 + (4 - 2) \div 2 + 6$$

A. 8.5

B. 12

C. 10

D. 1

**10** Which figure has 12 edges and 6 faces?

A. Rectangular prism

B. Rectangle

C. Triangular pyramid

D. Triangular prism

**11** Billy has a 15-gallon aquarium for his fish. Which metric unit of measure is best for calculating the volume of the tank?

A. Kilogram

B. Liter

C. Centimeter

D. Millimeter

**12** Which of the following would best be measured using square feet?

A. The weight of a snake

B. The height of a space shuttle

C. The area of a gym floor

D. The amount of gold in an Olympic medal

**GO ON**

**13** In a lottery, one winning ticket is drawn from a hat. If 50 tickets are sold and Hugh buys 3 tickets, what is the probability that he will win the lottery?

A. 0.1

B. $\frac{3}{10}$

C. 0.0333

D. 0.06

**14** There are 6 boys for every 11 girls in Deer Lakes High School. How many boys are there if there are 121 girls in the school?

A. 50

B. 66

C. 88

D. 111

**15** Which of the following figures has the most lines of symmetry?

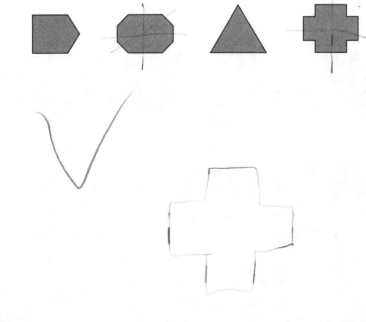

A. A

B. B

C. C

D. D

GO ON

**16** Which of the numbers below are in order from least to greatest?

A.  $-3, 0, -2, 2$

B.  $\frac{2}{3}, -4, 5, 6$

C.  .2, .02, 03, .5

D.  0.20, 28%, $\frac{34}{100}$, 65%

**17** If the image below is rotated clockwise 180 degrees what will the new image look like?

A.

B.

C.

D.

**GO ON**

**18** Mr. Flanders wants to buy a car that costs $1,200 and new tires that cost $150. He has $300. Which equation can be used to find $Z$, the amount of money still needed in order to buy both the car and the tires?

**A.** $Z = \$1200 + \$150 - \$300$

**B.** $Z = \$1200 - \$300$

**C.** $Z = \$1200 - \$150$

**D.** $Z = \$1200 + \$150 + \$300$

**19** Approximately 52 cars pass a red light every hour. About how many cars will pass the red light during the next 8 hours?

**A.** 60 cars

**B.** 300 cars

**C.** 400 cars

**D.** 600 cars

**20** The diameter of a circle is 6 centimeters. What would be the measurement of the circumference of the circle?

**A.** 10 cm

**B.** 15 cm

**C.** 19 cm

**D.** 22 cm

20/20

**GO ON**

291

# Part II   Extended Constructed-Response Questions

**Directions:** Write your answer neatly and clearly on the lines or in the space provided. Make sure to answer all of the parts of each question. The use of a calculator is permitted on this portion of the test.

**21** Question 21 refers to the cube below.

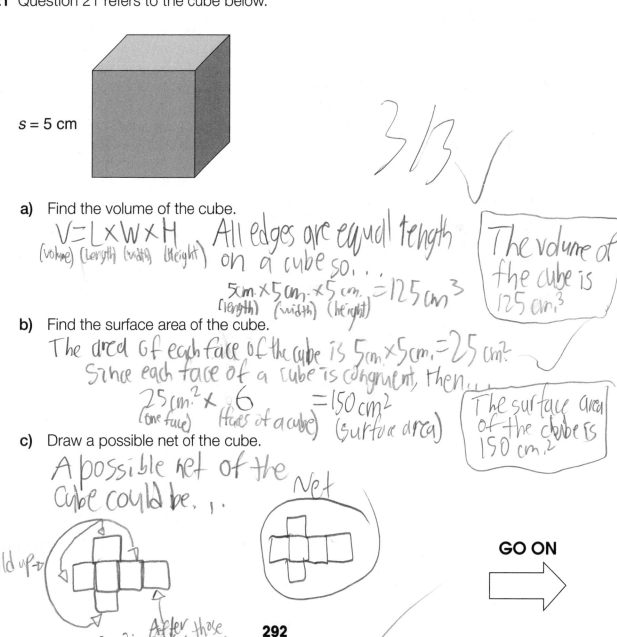

$s = 5$ cm

**a)** Find the volume of the cube.

V = L × W × H
(volume) (length) (width) (height)

All edges are equal length on a cube so...

5cm. × 5cm. × 5cm. = 125 cm³
(length) (width) (height)

The volume of the cube is 125 cm³

**b)** Find the surface area of the cube.

The area of each face of the cube is 5cm × 5cm. = 25 cm².
Since each face of a cube is congruent, then...
25 cm² × 6 = 150 cm²
(one face) (faces of a cube) (surface area)

The surface area of the cube is 150 cm.²

**c)** Draw a possible net of the cube.

A possible net of the cube could be...

Net

Step 1. Fold up →

Step 2: After those folding up, fold this up, fold this down to cover the open top

**292**

**GO ON**

**22** Question 22 refers to the table below that shows the temperature of a pot of water sitting on a stove.

| Time in seconds | Temperature of water (°F) |
|---|---|
| 5 s | 72 |
| 10 s | 95 |
| 15 s | 120 |
| 20 s | 145 |
| 25 s | ? |

**a)** How many degrees did the temperature of the water increase from 5 s until 20 s?

$72° + x = 145°$
(5 sec.)         (20 sec.)

$-72 + x = 145$
$-72 \qquad -72$
$x = 73$

The temperature increased 73° from 5 seconds until 20 seconds.

**b)** Estimate what temperature the water is after 25 s.

5–10 sec. – Rose 23° (72° to 95°)
10–15 sec. – Rose 25° (95° to 120°)
15–20 sec. – Rose 25° (120° to 145°)

$\frac{23 + 25 + 25}{3} = \frac{73}{3} = 24.3$ average rise in degrees per five seconds

$145° + 24.3 = 169.3$ is about 169°
(20 sec.)

**c)** Did the water temperature increase more from 5 s until 15 s or from 10 s until 20 s?

Increase

5s–15s: 72° to 120°
$120° - 72° = 48°$
increase

10s–2s = 95° to 145°
$145° - 95° = 50°$
increase

$50° > 48°$

so... The temperature of the water increased more from 10 seconds until 20 seconds than from 5 to 10.

After 25 seconds, the temperature will be about 169°F.

**STOP**

IF YOU HAVE TIME, YOU MAY REVIEW YOUR WORK IN THIS SECTION ONLY.

293

# Mathematics

This test is also on CD-ROM in our special interactive NJ ASK6 Mathematics TestWare®. It is highly recommended that you first take this exam on computer. You will then have the additional study features and benefits of enforced timed conditions and instant, accurate scoring.

**Directions to the Student**

*The New Jersey Assessment of Skills and Knowledge (ASK) is a test of how well you understand mathematics. The test consists of two different types of questions: multiple-choice and open-ended.*

**There are several things to remember:**

1. Read each question carefully and think about the answer. Then choose or write the answer that you think is best.

2. When you are asked to select the answer, make sure you circle the letter of the correct answer.

3. When you are asked to write your answers, write them neatly and clearly on the lines or in the space provided.

4. If you finish a part of the test early, you may check over your work in that part.

5. If you do not know the answer to a question, skip it and go on. You may return to it later if you have time.

**GO ON**

**MATHEMATICS REFERENCE SHEET**

The sum of the measures of the interior angles of a triangle = 180°

Distance = rate × time

Simple Interest Formula: $A = p + prt$

 $A$ = amount after t years; $p$ = principal; $r$ = annual interest rate; $t$ = number of years

---

$\pi = 3.14$ or $\frac{22}{7}$

**Square**
Area = $s^2$
Perimeter = $4s$

**Rectangle**
Area = $lw$
Perimeter = $2l + 2w$

**Circle**
Area = $\pi r^2$
Circumference = $2\pi r$
   = $\pi d$

**Triangle**
Area = $\frac{1}{2} bh$

**Parallelogram**
Area = $bh$

**Trapezoid**
Area = $\frac{1}{2} h(b_1 + b_2)$

**Rectangular Prism**
Volume = $lwh$
Surface Area =
   $2lw + 2wh + 2lh$

**Cylinder**
Volume = $\pi r^2 h$
Surface Area =
   $2\pi rh + 2\pi r^2$

---

### USE THE FOLLOWING EQUIVALENTS FOR YOUR CALCULATIONS

| | | |
|---|---|---|
| 60 seconds = 1 minute | 12 inches = 1 foot | 10 millimeters = 1 centimeter |
| 60 minutes = 1 hour | 3 feet = 1 yard | 100 centimeters = 1 meter |
| 24 hours = 1 day | 36 inches = 1 yard | 10 decimeters = 1 meter |
| 7 days = 1 week | 5,280 feet = 1 mile | 1000 meters = 1 kilometer |
| 12 months = 1 year | 1,760 yards = 1 mile | |
| 365 days = 1 year | | |

| | |
|---|---|
| 8 fluid ounces = 1 cup | 16 ounces = 1 pound |
| 2 cups = 1 pint | 2,000 pounds = 1 ton |
| 2 pints = 1 quart | |
| 4 quarts = 1 gallon | 1000 milligrams = 1 gram |
| | 100 centigrams = 1 gram |
| 1000 milliliters (mL) = 1 liter (L) | 10 grams = 1 dekagram |
| | 1000 grams = 1 kilogram |

**GO ON** →

**(Answer Sheets and a Mathematics Manipulative Sheet appear at the back of this book.)**

# Day 1
# Part I   Short Constructed-Response Questions

**Directions:** Solve each problem and write your answer on the answer sheet. No calculator is permitted on this portion of the test.

**1** If a t-shirt goes on sale for 25% off, how much is the discount on a T-shirt that originally costs $36.00?

$9   ✓

**2** How many miles does a person travel if she drives a car at 50 miles per hour for 3.5 hours?

175 miles   ✓

**3** If a 6-sided number cube is rolled twice, what is the probability that a 1 is rolled both times?

$$\frac{1}{36}$$   ✓

**4** If a sandwich shop sells lunches that include one sandwich and one side dish, draw a tree diagram to represent the number of combinations that are possible if the choices are a ham or turkey sandwich and chips or cookies as the side dish.

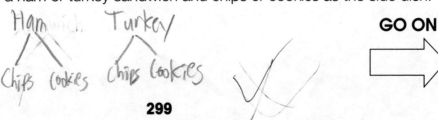

**GO ON** ⟹

299

**5** How many pounds does a 3.5-ton truck weigh?

7000 pounds ✓

**6** Fill in the appropriate inequality symbol.

15 liters $<$ 25 quarts

6/6

**GO ON** →

# Part II   Multiple-Choice Questions

**Directions:** Fill in the correct choice on the answer sheet. Calculators are permitted for this portion of the test.

**7** Amir asked 20 of his closest friends to tell him their favorite month of the year. July was the favorite month of the year for 75% of his friends. How many of his friends chose July?

   **A.**  10

   **B.**  12

   **(C.)**  15

   **D.**  18

**8** If the image below is reflected across the *x*-axis, how will it look after the reflection?

*Original*

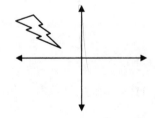

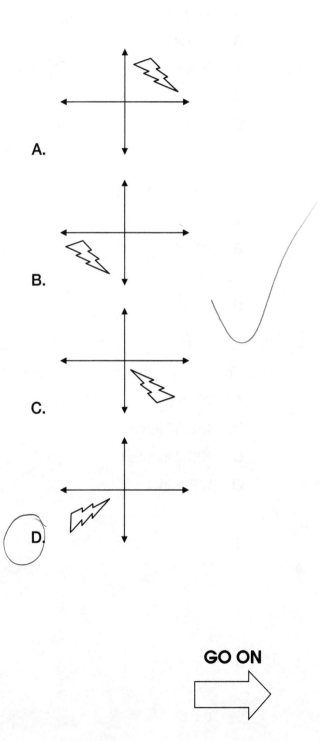

A.

B.

C.

D.

**9** A bowling-alley manager ordered 6 bowling balls. The heaviest ball weighed 15 lbs. The lightest ball weighed 6 lbs. What is a reasonable estimate of the weight of all six bowling balls?

   **A.** 25 lbs

   **B.** 36 lbs

   **C.** 63 lbs

   **D.** 95 lbs

**10** Evaluate $12.96 - 4.6 + 3.01$

   **A.** 11.46

   **B.** 20.57

   **C.** 11.91

   **D.** 11.37

**11** How many inches are in 3.7 yards?

   **A.** 79 inches

   **B.** 138.86 inches

   **C.** 133.2 inches

   **D.** 106.9 inches

**12** If the basketball team played 32 games, and Jason played in 28 games, what percentage of the games did Jason play in?

   **A.** 25%

   **B.** 50%

   **C.** 75%

   **D.** 88%

**13** Which ordered pair is located inside the rectangle but outside the circle?

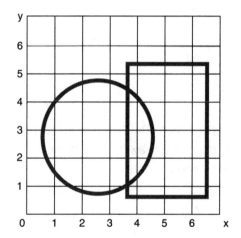

   **A.** (4, 2)

   **B.** (1, 1)

   **C.** (3, 4)

   **D.** (5, 3)

**GO ON**

**14** Which of the following statements is true?

   A.   Parallelograms are always rectangles.

   B.   Rhombuses and squares always have 4 congruent angles.

   C.   Rectangles and squares always have 4 congruent angles.

   D.   Rectangles and squares always have 4 congruent sides.

Questions 15–17 refer to the pie chart below.

**Favorite Vacation Places of Students in 6th Grade**

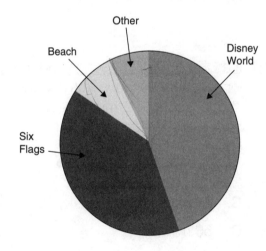

**15** Which of the following pairs total approximately 15% of the circle graph?

   A.   Six Flags and Beach

   B.   Disney World and Six Flags

   C.   Beach and Other

   D.   Other and Disney World

**16** If 500 students were asked where they liked to go on vacation, about how many said the beach?

   A.   10

   B.   40

   C.   70

   D.   100

**17** What is the approximate probability of picking a student at random whose favorite vacation spot is Six Flags?

   A.   0.3

   B.   0.5

   C.   0.7

   D.   0.9

**GO ON**

**18** What shape is congruent with the one below?

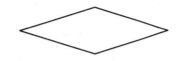

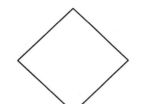

**A.**

**B.**

**C.**

**D.**

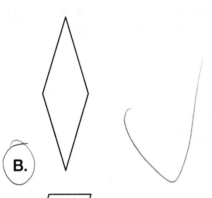

**19** Jim can run one lap at the track in 1.5 minutes. At this rate, how many minutes will it take Jim to run 4 laps?

A.   2 minutes

B.   4 minutes

C.   6 minutes

D.   8 minutes

**20** $6 \times 2 + 12 \div 4 - (4 + 3) =$

A.   8

B.   14

C.   24

D.   $-1$

**21** If a CD contains 15 songs and the longest song is 5 minutes and the shortest song is 2 minutes, about how many minutes long is the entire CD?

A.   20 minutes

B.   35 minutes

C.   50 minutes

D.   75 minutes

**GO ON**

# Part III   Extended Constructed-Response Question

**Directions:** Write your answer neatly and clearly on the lines or in the space provided. Make sure to answer all of the parts of each question. The use of a calculator is permitted on this portion of the test.

**22** Emily's recipe for one batch of cookies calls for 2.5 cups of flour.

a) How many cups of flour does Emily need to make $\frac{1}{2}$ a batch of cookies?

One batch is 2.5 cups

So... To make $\frac{1}{2}$ (which is one batch=2)
you divide one batch by 2 and 2.5 cups by 2. 0 2

1 batch ÷ $\frac{1}{2}$ batch
2.5 cups ÷ 2 1.25 cups

Emily needs 1.25 cups of flour for $\frac{1}{2}$ a batch of cookies

b) How many batches of cookies can she make with 7.5 cups of flour? Show how you got your answer.

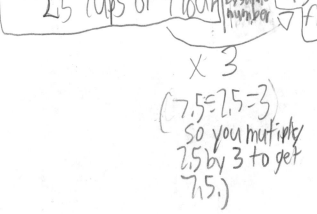

×3 → 3 batches

1 batch
2.5 cups of flour

Must also be multiplied by same number

X batches
7.5 cups of flour

Emily can make 3 batches of cookies with 7.5 cups of flowers

X 3

( 7.5 ÷ 2.5 = 3 )
So you mutiply 2.5 by 3 to get 7.5.

STOP

IF YOU HAVE TIME, YOU MAY REVIEW YOUR WORK IN THIS SECTION ONLY.

# Day 2

# Part I   Multiple-Choice Questions

**Directions:** Fill in the correct choice on the answer sheet. Calculators are permitted for this portion of the test.

1

Which inequality is graphed in the number line above?

A.  $x < -7$

B.  $x > -7$

C.  $x \leq -7$

D.  $x \geq -7$

2 What is 3 and forty-five thousandths written as a decimal?

A.   3.45

B.   3.045

C.   3.0045

D.   3,450

3 Which of the following fractions is the smallest?

A.   $\frac{2}{4}$

B.   $\frac{3}{10}$

C.   $\frac{11}{50}$

D.   $\frac{1}{6}$

**GO ON**

306

**4** How many vertices does this object have?

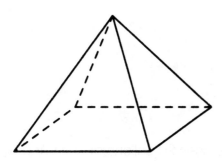

**A.** 8

**B.** 5

**C.** 3

**D.** 0

**5** What is the best estimate of the length of an adult human foot?

**A.** 10 mm

**B.** 1 m

**C.** 10 inches

**D.** 3 yards

**6**

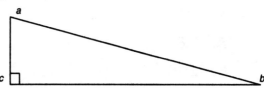

If angle $a = 70°$, what is the measure of angle $b$?

**A.** 10°

**B.** 20°

**C.** 50°

**D.** 90°

**7** What is the name for a polygon with 7 sides?

**A.** quadrilateral

**B.** hexagon

**C.** heptagon

**D.** decagon

**GO ON**

**8** In a field there are 10 bushes, 8 bales of hay, and 2 rock piles. What is the ratio of rock piles to bushes?

    **A.** 2:8

    **B.** 2:10

    **C.** 10:2

    **D.** 8:2

**9** Tom's boat has a 210-gallon tank for gas. If he uses 20 gallons of gas per day, about how many days will one tank of gas last?

    **A.** About 5 days

    **B.** About 10 days

    **C.** About 15 days

    **D.** About 20 days

**10** What fraction would 2.35 be equivalent to in simplest form?

    **A.** $2\frac{3}{5}$

    **B.** $2\frac{35}{100}$

    **C.** $2\frac{1}{5}$

    **D.** $2\frac{7}{20}$

**11** Which of the following has no vertices?

 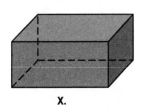 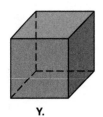 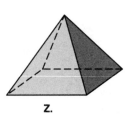

    **W.**        **X.**        **Y.**        **Z.**

**GO ON**

A. *W* and *X*

B. *W* only

C. *X, Y,* and *Z*

D. None. All of the shapes have vertices.

**12** Rebekah's mother gave her $35.00 to spend at the mall. Rebekah bought a shirt for $12.75 and a pair of shoes for $11.99. About how much money does Rebekah have left over?

A. $3.00

B. $10.00

C. $17.00

D. $28.00

**13** The first five terms in a sequence are written below.

$$3, 12, 21, 30, 39$$

What is the next term?

A. 41

B. 45

C. 48

D. 51

**14** Which of the angles below are acute angles?

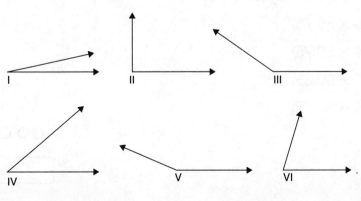

**GO ON**

**A.** I and II

**B.** I, IV, and V

**C.** III and V

**D.** I, IV, and VI

**15** If Jack bought a car new for $20,000.00 and Jim bought the same car two years later for $12,000.00, what percent of the original price did Jim pay?

**A.** 30%

**B.** 50%

**C.** 60%

**D.** 90%

**16** Which expression can be used to show how the distributive property can be used to multiply the following numbers?

$$3 \times 2.65$$

**A.** $3(2 - 0.65)$

**B.** $3 + (2 + 0.65)$

**C.** $3 - (2 + 0.65)$

**D.** $3(2 + 0.65)$

**17** Barbie bought 4 apples at $0.35 per apple and 5 oranges at $0.75 per orange. Which equation gives the total cost (C) of the fruit?

**A.** $C = (4 \times \$0.35) + (5 \times \$0.75)$

**B.** $C = (5 \times \$0.35) + (4 \times \$0.75)$

**C.** $C = (4 + \$0.75) \times (5 + \$0.35)$

**D.** $C = (4 - \$0.35) \times (5 - \$0.75)$

**GO ON**

**18** Which type of transformation is shown below?

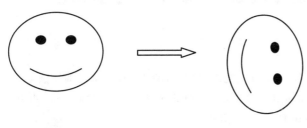

    **A.**  Reflection

    **B.**  Rotation

    **C.**  Translation

    **D.**  Expansion

**19** Alyson is looking at a map of the United States. On the map, New York City, New York, is 4 inches from Pittsburgh, Pennsylvenia. If the true distance between New York City and Pittsburgh is 400 miles, what is the scale of the map?

    **A.**  1 inch = 200 miles

    **B.**  1 inch = 100 miles

    **C.**  1 inch = 400 miles

    **D.**  1 inch = 50 miles

**20** Convert to pounds: 6.5 tons

    **A.**  6,500 lbs

    **B.**  10,000 lbs

    **C.**  13,000 lbs

    **D.**  65,000 lbs

20/20

**GO ON**

# Part II   Extended Constructed Response Questions

**Directions:** Write your answer neatly and clearly on the lines or in the space provided. Make sure to answer all of the parts of each question. The use of a calculator is permitted on this portion of the test.

3/3

21  Steven wants to buy some video games that are on sale at a video outlet store for $6.50 each. He found the same video games on the Internet for $3 each. However, on the Internet, he must pay a handling fee of $2 for any order and an additional $1.50 in shipping for each video game. If Steven wants to buy 10 video games, should he buy them at the store or on the Internet? Explain your answer and show your work.

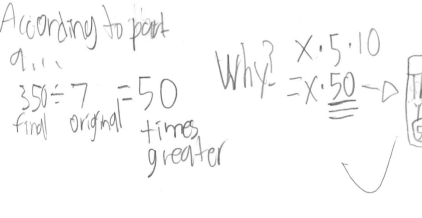

Store
10 games × $6.50 each = $65.00 total

Internet
10 games × ($3 + $1.50) + $2 = 10 × $4.50 + 2 = $47 total
each   shipping   for order (10 or more ordered)

So...
$65 > $47
Store   Internet
(He should buy them on the Internet.)   ✓

22  Todd told his friends about a special function. The first number is multiplied by 5 and then the product is multiplied by 10.

a)  What would the final number be if 7 were used?

7 × 5 = 35
35 × 10 = 350

The final number would be 350.   ✓

b)  How many times greater is the final answer than the original number?

According to part a...
350 ÷ 7 = 50
final   original   times greater

Why? x · 5 · 10 = x · 50 ─▷

The final number must always be 50 times greater than the original number.   ✓

**STOP**

IF YOU HAVE TIME, YOU MAY REVIEW YOUR WORK IN THIS SECTION ONLY.

# Practice Test 1

# Answer Key

## Day 1

### Part I

See Detailed Explanations of Answers

### Part II

7. A
8. A
9. B
10. C
11. C
12. D
13. D
14. C
15. A
16. C
17. B
18. D
19. D
20. C
21. A

### Part III

See Detailed Explanations of Answers

## Day 2

### Part I

1. C
2. C
3. A
4. D
5. A
6. D
7. D
8. D
9. C
10. A
11. B
12. C
13. D
14. B
15. C
16. D
17. D
18. A
19. C
20. C

### Part II

See Detailed Explanations of Answers

# Practice Test 1

## Detailed Explanations of Answers

### Day 1
### Part I

**1.** (Standard Assessed: Geometry and Measurement)
$V = \pi r^2 h = \pi(4^2)(10) = 160\pi$ cubic inches.

**2.** (Standard Assessed: Geometry and Measurement)
The triangular prism has 9 edges.

**3.** (Standard Assessed: Data Analysis, Probability and Discrete Mathematics)

$$P(Black\ Marble) = \frac{number\ of\ black\ marbles}{total\ number\ of\ marbles} = \frac{2}{11}$$

**4.** (Standard Assessed: Geometry and Measurement)
$p = 2l + 2w = 2(8) = 2(5) = 26$ ft.

**5.** (Standard Assessed: Number and Numerical Operations)
$448.6 \div 49.2 \approx 450 \div 50 = 9$.

**6.** (Standard Assessed: Patterns, Algebra and Functions)
$3 - (1 + 2) \times 6 = 3 - 3 \times 6 = 3 - 18 = -15$.

## Part II

**7. A** (Standard Assessed: Number and Numerical Operations)

To solve this problem, combine the three results of the plays.

$+35 - 6 - 3 = +26$ yards.

Choice B is wrong because it treats all the numbers as positives instead of positive and negative. Choice C is wrong because it ignores the $-6$ and choice D is wrong because it treats all the numbers as negatives instead of positive and negative.

**8  A** (Standard Assessed: Patterns, Algebra and Functions)

The two negatives become positive and then you should subtract 8 from both sides of the equation. Choice B is wrong because it adds 8 to both sides of the equation. Choices C and D are wrong by arithmetic error.

**9. B** (Standard Assessed: Patterns, Algebra and Functions)

Each number is multiplied by 2 to produce the next number. Choice A is wrong because $4 \div 2$ is not 8. Choice C is wrong because $8 - (-4)$ is not 16. Choice D is wrong because $4 + 16$ is not 8.

**10. C** (Standard Assessed: Number and Numerical Operations)

$6.75 - 3.175 = 3.575$. Choice A is wrong because it treats 6.75 as a negative number. Choice B is wrong because it subtracts the two numbers in the wrong order. Choice D is wrong because it adds the two numbers.

**11. C** (Standard Assessed: Number and Numerical Operations)

$\frac{2}{3} + 2\frac{2}{3} = 3\frac{1}{3}$ . Choice A is wrong because $\frac{1}{2} + 1\frac{1}{2} = 2$ . Choice B is wrong because $\frac{3}{4} + \frac{3}{4} = 1\frac{1}{2}$. Choice D is wrong because $\frac{4}{3} + 1\frac{1}{3} = 2\frac{2}{3}$.

**12. D** (Standard Assessed: Number and Numerical Operations)

To find the average price, divide the price by the number of sticks of bubble gum, ($3.55 \div 40 = 0.008875$), which rounds to the nearest cent as $0.09. Choices A and B are wrong by arithmetic error. Choice C is wrong due to a rounding error.

**13. D**   (Standard Assessed: Data Analysis, Probability and Discrete Mathematics)

The range is the difference between the highest and lowest scores, so if the range is 41 and the lowest grade is 58, the highest grade is $58 + 41 = 99$. Choice A is wrong because it subtracts $58 - 41$. Choice B is wrong because it does not take the range into account. Choice C is wrong by arithmetic error.

**14. C**   (Standard Assessed: Geometry and Measurement)

The sum of the measures of all three angles in a triangle is 180 degrees, so if the sum of two angles measures 120 degrees, the third angle must be $180 - 120 = 60$ degrees. Choice A is wrong because 240 is greater than 180. Choice B is wrong because $120 + 90$ does not equal 180 and choice D is wrong because $120 + 30$ also does not equal 180.

**15. A**   (Standard Assessed: Geometry and Measurement)

A regular pentagon has one line of symmetry for each vertex. Choice B is wrong because a pentagon does not have 6 vertices. Choice C is wrong because a regular pentagon does not have 8 vertices. Choice D is wrong because a regular pentagon does have symmetry.

**16. C**   (Standard Assessed: Data Analysis, Probability and Discrete Mathematics)

We use the multiplication counting principle to multiply the number of ice cream flavors and the number of choices for cones, thus, $2 \times 2 = 4$. Choices A and B are wrong because they do not use the Multiplication Counting Principle. Choice D is wrong by arithmetic error.

**17. B**   (Standard Assessed: Geometry and Measurement)

The formula for the area of a triangle is $A = \frac{1}{2}bh$. $(0.5)(4)(6) = 12$ square inches. Choice A is wrong because it adds the base and height instead of using the correct formula. Choice C is wrong because it does not multiply by $\frac{1}{2}$ and choice D is wrong by arithmetic error.

**18. D**   (Standard Assessed: Geometry and Measurement)

A bathtub could easily hold 20 gallons. Choice A is wrong because a dinner glass cannot hold even one gallon of milk. Choice B is wrong because a milk jug is only one gallon or less. Choice C is wrong because a flower pot could not hold much more than a milk jug.

**19. D**  (Standard Assessed: Number and Numerical Operations)

To find the LCD, we multiply the prime factorization of 5 and 6, which is $5 \times 2 \times 3 = 30$. Choice A is wrong because 5 is not a multiple of 6. Choice B is wrong because 6 is not a multiple of 5. Choice C is wrong because 11 is neither a multiple of 5 nor 6.

**20. C**  (Standard Assessed: Geometry and Measurement)

A box is a rectangular prism. Choice A is wrong because a tent is usually shaped like a triangular prism. Choice B is wrong because a soda can is shaped like a cylinder. Choice D is wrong because a candle is also shaped like a cylinder.

**21. A**  (Standard Assessed: Number and Numerical Operations)

100 lbs. weighs the least after all of the choices are converted to pounds. Choice B is wrong because 0.25 tons = 500 pounds. Choice C is wrong because 2,000 pounds is clearly greater than 100 pounds. Choice D is wrong because 2,000,000 oz. = 125,000 lbs.

# Part III

**22.** (Standard Assessed: Data Analysis, Probability and Discrete Mathematics)

    a)  The shortest distance from home to work is $3 + 4 = 7$ miles.

    b)  The round trip home-school-pool-home is $6 + 5 + 3 = 14$ miles.

    c)  The shortest trip from work to school $= 4 + 5 = 9$ miles. The shortest trip from the church to the pool $= 6 + 4 = 10$ miles, so church to pool is the longer trip.

# Day 2

## Part I    Multiple-Choice Questions

**1. C**  (Standard Assessed: Geometry and Measurement)

It is very important that a surgeon make a precise cut and the difference in surgery between a three-millimeter cut and a three-inch cut is significant. Choice A is wrong because the amount of time it takes to shower can be measured in minutes without a need for greater accuracy. Choice B is wrong because the temperature does not need to be measured with greater accuracy than simple degrees. Choice D is wrong because the amount of time to drive to school can be measured in minutes without a need for greater accuracy.

**2. C**   (Standard Assessed: Patterns, Algebra and Functions)

Since David has $4.50 and laps are sold in groups of $0.50, we divide $4.50 by $0.50 = 9. Thus, David can buy 9 sets of five laps. To find out how many laps that is, we multiply $9 \times 5$. Choice A is wrong because it adds 9 and 5. Choice B is wrong because it subtracts 5 from 9. Choice D is wrong because it is 9 divided by 5.

**3. A**   (Standard Assessed: Patterns, Algebra and Functions)

To find profit, we subtract price − expenses, so Jason's profit is $234.91 − $65.71 = $169.20. Choice B is wrong because it adds the sale price and expenses. Choice C is wrong by arithmetic error. Choice D is wrong because it does not consider the cost of the parts of the engine.

**4. D**   (Standard Assessed: Patterns, Algebra and Functions)

Add 39 to both sides of the equation. Choice A is wrong because it multiplies 147 by 39. Choice B is wrong because it divides 147 by 39. Choice C is wrong because it subtracts 39 from 147.

**5. A**   (Standard Assessed: Patterns, Algebra and Functions)

Substitute in 20 for $y$ and 6 for $z$ and the equation becomes $20 - 3(6) = 20 - 18 = 2$. Choice B is wrong by arithmetic error. Choice C is wrong by substitution error and arithmetic error. Choice D is wrong by arithmetic error.

**6. D**   (Standard Assessed: Number and Numerical Operations)

Divide 600 by 25. Choices A, B, and C are all wrong by arithmetic error.

**7. D**   (Standard Assessed: Number and Numerical Operations)

To find the decimal equivalent of a fraction, divide the numerator by the denominator. $7 \div 8 = 0.875$. Choice A is wrong because $7 \div 8$ is not 0.5. Choice B is wrong because $7 \div 8$ is not 1.875. Choice C is wrong because $7 \div 8$ is not 1.5.

8. **D**   (Standard Assessed: Data Analysis, Probability and Discrete Mathematics)

   We list all the possibilities: Maggie and James, Maggie and Heath, Maggie and Sylvia, James and Heath, James and Sylvia, and Heath and Sylvia. Choice A is wrong because it does not consider all combinations of students. Choice B is wrong because it does not consider all combinations of students. Choice C is wrong because it does not consider all combinations of students.

9. **C**   (Standard Assessed: Number and Numerical Operations)

   Solve this problem by following the order of operations. $3 + (4 - 2) \div 2 + 6 = 3 + 2 \div 2 + 6 = 3 + 1 + 6 = 4 + 6 = 10$. Choice A is wrong because it solves the problem from left to right instead of using the order of operations. Choices B and D are wrong because of arithmetic errors and not following the order of operations.

10. **A**   (Standard Assessed: Geometry and Measurement)

    A rectangular prism is the only 6-sided (each side being a face) figure in the list. Choice B is wrong because a rectangle is a two-dimensional figure and does not have faces or edges. Choice C is wrong because a triangular pyramid has four faces. Choice D is wrong because a triangular prism has 5 faces.

11. **B**   (Standard Assessed: Geometry and Measurement)

    Liters are the only measure in the list that measures capacity. Choice A is wrong because kilograms measure weight. Choice C is wrong because centimeters measure length. Choice D is wrong because millimeters measure length.

12. **C**   (Standard Assessed: Geometry and Measurement)

    Square feet is a measure of area and choice C is the only choice that involves area. Choice A is wrong because weight should be measured in pounds. Choice B is wrong because height should be measured in feet, yards, or miles and Choice D is wrong because amount of gold is not measured in square feet.

13. **D**   (Standard Assessed: Data Analysis, Probability and Discrete Mathematics)

    Hugh has a $3 \div 50 = 0.06$ chance of winning the lottery. Choice A is wrong by arithmetic error. Choice B is wrong by arithmetic error. Choice C is wrong by arithmetic error.

**14. B**  (Standard Assessed: Number and Numerical Operations)

Set up the proportion $\frac{6}{11} = \frac{\square}{121}$ . Since $11 \times 11 = 121$, we have to multiply $6 \times 11$ = 66. Choices A, C, and D are wrong by arithmetic error.

**15. C**  (Standard Assessed: Geometry and Measurement)

The regular triangle has 3 lines of symmetry. Choice A has only one line of symmetry. Choice B has only two lines of symmetry and choice D has only two lines of symmetry.

**16. D**  (Standard Assessed: Number and Numerical Operations)

After changing all of the numbers into decimal form, $0.20 < 0.28 < 0.34 < 0.65$. Choice A is wrong because 0 is not less than $-2$. Choice B is wrong because $\frac{2}{3}$ is not less than $-4$. Choice C is wrong because 0.2 is not less than 0.02.

**17. D**  (Standard Assessed: Geometry and Measurement)

A rotation of 180 degrees "flips" the image vertically. Choice A is not rotation at all. Choice B is a rotation of 90 degrees counterclockwise. Choice C is a rotation of 270 degrees counterclockwise.

**18. A**  (Standard Assessed: Patterns, Algebra and Functions)

$1200 + 150$ represents the cost of the car and tires, $-300$ represents the amount of money Mr. Flanders currently has, so the amount of money he needs is $1200 + 150 - 300$. Choice B neglects the cost of the tires. Choice C neglects the amount of money Mr. Flanders has saved. Choice D adds the amount of money saved instead of subtracting it.

**19. C**  (Standard Assessed: Number and Numerical Operations)

We estimate the product of 52 and 8 by using $50 \times 8 = 400$. Choice A is wrong because that is the number of cars in one hour, not 8. Choice B is wrong by arithmetic error. Choice D is wrong by arithmetic error.

**20. C**  (Standard Assessed: Geometry and Measurement)

The circumference of a circle is found by multiplying the diameter by $\pi$. $C = (3.14)(6) = 19$ cm. Choice A is wrong by arithmetic error.  Choices B and D are also wrong by arithmetic error.

## Part II

**21.** (Standard Assessed: Geometry and Measurement)

a) $V = s^2 = 5^2 = 125$ cubic cm.

b) $SA = 2lw + 2lh + 2wh = 2(5)(5) + 2(5)(5) + 2(5)(5) =$
   $50 + 50 + 50 = 150$ square cm.

c)

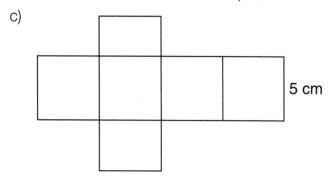

5 cm

**22.** (Standard Assessed: Number and Numerical Operations)

a) $145 - 72 = 73°F$.

b) Since the pattern shows that the temperature increased by 23, 25, and 25 degrees during the previous 5 s intervals, a good estimate is to expect another 25-degree increase in water temperature. So, the water temperature after 25 s is approximately 170°F.

c) The increase from 5 s until 15 s is $120 - 72 = 48$ degrees. The increase from 10 s until 20 s is $145 - 95 = 50$ degrees. So, the water temperature increased more from 10 s until 20 s.

# Practice Test 2

# Answer Key

## Day 1

### Part I

See Detailed Explanations of Answers

### Part II

7. C
8. D
9. C
10. D
11. C
12. D
13. D
14. C
15. C
16. B
17. B
18. B
19. C
20. A
21. C

### Part III

See Detailed Explanations of Answers

## Day 2

### Part I

1. D
2. B
3. D
4. B
5. C
6. B
7. C
8. B
9. B
10. D
11. B
12. B
13. C
14. D
15. C
16. D
17. A
18. B
19. B
20. C

### Part II

See Detailed Explanations of Answers

# Practice Test 2

# Detailed Explanations of Answers

## Day 1

## Part I

1. (Standard Assessed: Patterns, Algebra and Functions)

   $\$36.00 \times 25\% = 36 \times 0.25 = \$9.00$. The discount is 9 dollars.

2. (Standard Assessed: Patterns, Algebra and Functions)

   $$50\,\frac{miles}{hour} \times 3.5\,hours = 175\,miles$$

3. (Standard Assessed: Data Analysis, Probability and Discrete Mathematics)

   $$P(rolling\ a\ 1) \times P(rolling\ a\ 1) = \frac{1}{6} \times \frac{1}{6} = \frac{1}{36}$$

4. (Standard Assessed: Data Analysis, Probability and Discrete Mathematics)

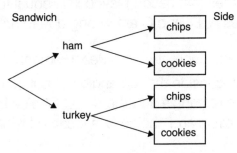

5. (Standard Assessed: Geometry and Measurement)

   $3.5 \times 2000 = 7{,}000$ pounds

6. (Standard Assessed: Geometry and Measurement)

   15 liters __≤__ 25 quarts

## Part II

**7. C**   (Standard Assessed: Number and Numerical Operations)

Multiply $20 \times 0.75 = 15$. Choice A is 50% of 20. Choice B is 60% of 20. Choice D is 90% of 20.

**8. D**   (Standard Assessed: Geometry and Measurement)

A reflection over the x-axis "flips" the figure vertically. Choices A and B are translations. Choice C is a rotation of 180 degrees about the origin.

**9. C**   (Standard Assessed: Number and Numerical Operations)

Since the heaviest ball plus the lightest ball weighs 21 pounds ($15 + 6 = 21$), we multiply $21 \times 3 = 63$ pounds as an estimate since there are 6 bowling balls. Choices A and B are far too light since only two balls together weigh 21 pounds. Choice D is too heavy since the heaviest any ball can be is 15 pounds.

**10. D**   (Standard Assessed: Number and Numerical Operations)

$12.96 - 4.6 + 3.01 = 8.36 + 3.01 = 11.37$. Choice A is wrong due to lining up the decimal point incorrectly. Choice B is wrong due to adding 4.6 instead of subtracting 4.6. Choice C is wrong due to arithmetic error.

**11. C**   (Standard Assessed: Geometry and Measurement)

Since there are 36 inches in 1 yard, there are $36 \times 3.7 = 133.2$ inches in 3.7 yards. All the other choices are wrong due to conversion/arithmetic errors.

**12. D**   (Standard Assessed: Number and Numerical Operations)

The percentage of games that Jason played in is equal to $28 \div 32 \times 100\% = 87.5\% \approx 88\%$. Choices A, B, and C are wrong due to arithmetic errors.

**13. D**   (Standard Assessed: Geometry and Measurement)

(5, 3) is the point located inside the rectangle but outside the circle. Choice A is located inside both the rectangle and the circle. Choice B is located outside both the rectangle and the circle and choice C is located inside the circle but outside the rectangle.

**14. C**   (Standard Assessed: Geometry and Measurement)

Rectangles and squares always have four 90° angles. Choice A is wrong because a parallelogram does not have to have four 90° angles, but a rectangle does. Choice B is wrong because rhombuses are not required to have 4 congruent angles. Choice D is wrong because rectangles do not have to have 4 congruent sides.

**15. C** (Standard Assessed: Data Analysis, Probability and Discrete Mathematics)

The Beach and Other together total approximately 15% of the graph. Choice A is wrong because Six Flags and the Beach total more than 50%. Choice B is wrong because Disney World and Six Flags total more than 50%. Choice D is wrong because Disney World and Other total approximately 33%.

**16. B** (Standard Assessed: Data Analysis, Probability and Discrete Mathematics),

Multiply $500 \times 7.5\% = 500 \times 0.75$, which is approximately 40. The other choices are wrong by arithmetic errors.

**17. B** (Standard Assessed: Number and Numerical Operations; Data Analysis, Probability and Discrete Mathematics)

We estimate that the size of the Six Flags pie slice is 0.5, since it is about half of the pie graph. Choice A is far too small. Choice C is too large since $0.7 = 70\%$ is more than half of the pie graph and choice D is too large.

**18. B** (Standard Assessed: Geometry and Measurement)

The figure is the same size and shape, only rotated. Choices A, C and D are each the wrong size and shape.

**19. C** (Standard Assessed: Number and Numerical Operations)

Multiply $1.5 \times 4 = 6$ minutes to find how long 4 laps will take at 1.5 minutes per lap. Choices A and B are far too small. Choice D is the time it would take if Jim ran one lap in 2 minutes.

**20. A** (Standard Assessed: Number and Numerical Operations)

Follow the order of operations:
$6 \times 2 + 12 \div 4 - (4 + 3) = 6 \times 2 + 12 \div 4 - 7 = 12 + 12 \div 4 - 7 = 12 + 3 - 7 = 15 - 7 = 8$
Choices B, C, and D do not follow the order of operations.

**21. C** (Standard Assessed: Number and Numerical Operations)

The sum of the longest and shortest song is $5 + 2 = 7$ minutes. We can estimate the length of the CD by multiplying this sum by 7.5, since there were 15 songs total. $7 \times 7.5 = 52.5$ minutes $\approx 50$ minutes.

## Part III   Extended Constructed-Response Question

**22.** (Standard Assessed: Patterns, Algebra and Functions)

a) $2.5 \times \dfrac{1}{2} = 1.25$

b) $7.5 \div 2.5 = 3$. Emily has enough flour to make 3 batches of cookies.

## Day 2

## Part I   Multiple-Choice Questions

**1. D** (Standard Assessed: Patterns, Algebra and Functions)

Since the arrow is pointing to the right and the circle is filled in above $-7$, the inequality represents all values greater than or equal to ($\geq$) $-7$. Choice A refers to an arrow pointing left with an open circle over $-7$. Choice B refers to an arrow pointing right with an open circle over $-7$ and choice C refers to an arrow pointing left with a filled in circle over $-7$.

**2. B** (Standard Assessed: Number and Numerical Operations)

3 and forty-five thousandths means that there is a decimal point after 3 and that there is a 0 in the tenths place, a 4 in the hundredths place, and a 5 in the thousandths place (3.045). Choice A is 3 and forty-five hundredths. Choice C is 3 and forty-five ten-thousandths. Choice D is three-thousand four-hundred fifty.

**3. D** (Standard Assessed: Number and Numerical Operations)

$\dfrac{1}{6}$ is the smallest fraction. Compare the fractions by converting each to a decimal. Choice A is 0.5. Choice B is 0.3. Choice C is 0.22 and choice D is 0.167. Clearly, choice D is the smallest fraction.

**4. B** (Standard Assessed: Geometry and Measurement)

A vertex is a point where three or more edges come together. Choice A is too large. Choice C does not count all of the vertices and choice D does not count any vertices.

**5. C** (Standard Assessed: Geometry and Measurement)

One foot is equal to 12 inches, thus 10 inches is a good estimate. Choice A is far too short as 10 mm is closer to the width of a human finger. Choice B is far too large as 1 m is longer than 1 yard, which equals 36 inches. Choice D is too large since if one yard = 36 inches, 3 yards is clearly too long.

**6. B** (Standard Assessed: Geometry and Measurement)

The sum of measures of the three angles of a triangle is 180°. Since this is a right triangle and one angle is 70 degrees that means the sum of the two known angles is $90 + 70 = 160$. $180 - 160 = 20$ degrees. Choice A is too small. Choices C and D give a total angle measure greater than 180 degrees.

**7. C** (Standard Assessed: Geometry and Measurement)

A heptagon has 7 sides. Choice A is a quadrilateral which has 4 sides. Choice B is a hexagon which has 6 sides. Choice D is a decagon which has 10 sides.

**8. B** (Standard Assessed: Number and Numerical Operations)

There are 2 rock piles for every 10 bushes. Choice A is the ratio of rock piles to bales of hay. Choice C is the ratio of bushes to rock piles. Choice D is the ratio of bales of hay to rock piles.

**9. B** (Standard Assessed: Data Analysis, Probability and Discrete Mathematics)

We estimate how long one tank of gas will last by dividing $200 \div 20 = 10$. Choice A requires Tom to burn 40 gallons of gas per day. Choice C is an arithmetic error. Choice D requires Tom to burn only 10 gallons of gas per day.

**10. D** (Standard Assessed: Number and Numerical Operations)

Change 2.35 into the fraction $2\dfrac{35}{100}$ and then reduce the numerator and

denominator by 5 to get $2\dfrac{7}{20}$. Choice A is an arithmetic error in reducing. Choice B is not in reduced form. Choice C is an arithmetic error in reducing.

**11. B** (Standard Assessed: Geometry and Measurement)

A vertex is a point where at least 3 edges meet. The cylinder does not have any points where three edges meet. Choice A is wrong because the rectangular prism has 8 vertices. Choice C is wrong because all three shapes have vertices. Choice D is wrong because the cylinder does not have any vertices.

**12. B** (Standard Assessed: Patterns, Algebra and Functions)

Estimate the cost of the shirt as $13 and the cost of the shoes as $12, so Rebekah has $35 - 13 - 12 = 22 - 12 = \$10$ left over. Choices A, C, and D all show arithmetic errors.

**13. C** (Standard Assessed: Patterns, Algebra and Functions)

The rule/pattern is to add 9, so the next term is $39 + 9 = 48$. Choice A adds 3 instead of 9. Choice B adds 6 instead of 9 and choice D adds 12 instead of 9.

**14. D** (Standard Assessed: Geometry and Measurement)

An acute angle is an angle that is less than 90°. Angles I, IV, and VI are clearly smaller than a right angle. Choice A is wrong because angle II is a right angle. Choice B is wrong because angle V is an obtuse angle. Choice C is wrong because angles III and V are both obtuse angles.

**15. C** (Standard Assessed: Number and Numerical Operations)

To find the percent of the original price, divide the new price by the original price. So, Jim paid $12000 \div 20000 = 0.60 = 60\%$ of the original price.

**16. D** (Standard Assessed: Patterns, Algebra and Functions)

The distributive property means that addition can be done before multiplication if the multiplication is applied to the sum. Choice A is wrong because $2 - 0.65 \neq 2.65$. Choice B is wrong because it adds the 3 to the sum instead of multiplying the 3 and the sum. Choice C is wrong because it subtracts the sum from 3 instead of multiplying the 3 and the sum.

**17. A** (Standard Assessed: Patterns, Algebra and Functions)

To find the cost, multiply the number of apples times the price of one apple and add that to the price of one orange times the number of oranges. Choice B is wrong because it multiplies the number of oranges times the price of the apples and the number of apples times the price of the oranges. Choices C and D are wrong because they multiply the cost of the apples and oranges.

**18. B** (Standard Assessed: Geometry and Measurement)

A rotation is when the figure is "turned." Choice A is a reflection, which means that the figure must be "flipped" over some line. Choice C is a translation, which means the figure is left in its original orientation, but slid to a different place. Choice D is an expansion, which means that the figure is enlarged.

**19. B** (Standard Assessed: Geometry and Measurement)

To find the length of the scale, divide the true distance by the map distance. Thus, the scale of the map $= 400 \div 4 = 100$ miles per 1 inch. Choices A and C are too large a scale and choice D is too small a scale.

**20. C**   (Standard Assessed: Geometry and Measurement)

To convert tons into pounds, multiply the number of tons by 2000. So, $6.5 \times 2000$ = 13,000 pounds. Choices A and D use incorrect conversion rates and choice B is an arithmetic error.

## Part II   Extended Constructed Response Questions

**21.** (Standard Assessed: Patterns, Algebra and Functions; Data Analysis, Probability and Discrete Mathematics)

Cost of Video Games at the Store: $\$6.50 \times 10 = \$65.00$.

Cost of Video Games on the Internet: $\$3.00 \times 10 + \$2 + \$1.50 \times 10 = \$30 + \$2 + \$15 = \$32 + \$15 = \$47.00$.

Steven should buy the video games on the Internet since it will save him $18.00.

**22.** a)  (Standard Assessed: Data Analysis, Probability and Discrete Mathematics)

$(7 \times 5) \times 10 = 35 \times 10 = 350$

b)  (Standard Assessed: Patterns, Algebra and Functions)

$350 \div 7 = 50$. Thus, the final answer is 50 times greater than the original number.

# Practice Test 1

# Answer Sheet

**Day 1**

**Part I**

1. _____
2. _____
3. _____
4. _____
5. _____
6. _____

**Part II**

7. Ⓐ Ⓑ Ⓒ Ⓓ
8. Ⓐ Ⓑ Ⓒ Ⓓ
9. Ⓐ Ⓑ Ⓒ Ⓓ
10. Ⓐ Ⓑ Ⓒ Ⓓ
11. Ⓐ Ⓑ Ⓒ Ⓓ
12. Ⓐ Ⓑ Ⓒ Ⓓ
13. Ⓐ Ⓑ Ⓒ Ⓓ
14. Ⓐ Ⓑ Ⓒ Ⓓ
15. Ⓐ Ⓑ Ⓒ Ⓓ
16. Ⓐ Ⓑ Ⓒ Ⓓ
17. Ⓐ Ⓑ Ⓒ Ⓓ
18. Ⓐ Ⓑ Ⓒ Ⓓ
19. Ⓐ Ⓑ Ⓒ Ⓓ
20. Ⓐ Ⓑ Ⓒ Ⓓ
21. Ⓐ Ⓑ Ⓒ Ⓓ

**Part III**

22. See test page

**Day 2**

**Part I**

1. Ⓐ Ⓑ Ⓒ Ⓓ
2. Ⓐ Ⓑ Ⓒ Ⓓ
3. Ⓐ Ⓑ Ⓒ Ⓓ
4. Ⓐ Ⓑ Ⓒ Ⓓ
5. Ⓐ Ⓑ Ⓒ Ⓓ
6. Ⓐ Ⓑ Ⓒ Ⓓ
7. Ⓐ Ⓑ Ⓒ Ⓓ
8. Ⓐ Ⓑ Ⓒ Ⓓ
9. Ⓐ Ⓑ Ⓒ Ⓓ
10. Ⓐ Ⓑ Ⓒ Ⓓ
11. Ⓐ Ⓑ Ⓒ Ⓓ
12. Ⓐ Ⓑ Ⓒ Ⓓ
13. Ⓐ Ⓑ Ⓒ Ⓓ
14. Ⓐ Ⓑ Ⓒ Ⓓ
15. Ⓐ Ⓑ Ⓒ Ⓓ
16. Ⓐ Ⓑ Ⓒ Ⓓ
17. Ⓐ Ⓑ Ⓒ Ⓓ
18. Ⓐ Ⓑ Ⓒ Ⓓ
19. Ⓐ Ⓑ Ⓒ Ⓓ
20. Ⓐ Ⓑ Ⓒ Ⓓ

**Part II**

21. See test page
22. See test page

# Practice Test 2

## Answer Sheet

### Day 1

**Part I**

1. _____
2. _____
3. _____
4. _____
5. _____
6. _____

**Part II**

7. Ⓐ Ⓑ Ⓒ Ⓓ
8. Ⓐ Ⓑ Ⓒ Ⓓ
9. Ⓐ Ⓑ Ⓒ Ⓓ
10. Ⓐ Ⓑ Ⓒ Ⓓ
11. Ⓐ Ⓑ Ⓒ Ⓓ
12. Ⓐ Ⓑ Ⓒ Ⓓ
13. Ⓐ Ⓑ Ⓒ Ⓓ
14. Ⓐ Ⓑ Ⓒ Ⓓ
15. Ⓐ Ⓑ Ⓒ Ⓓ
16. Ⓐ Ⓑ Ⓒ Ⓓ
17. Ⓐ Ⓑ Ⓒ Ⓓ
18. Ⓐ Ⓑ Ⓒ Ⓓ
19. Ⓐ Ⓑ Ⓒ Ⓓ
20. Ⓐ Ⓑ Ⓒ Ⓓ
21. Ⓐ Ⓑ Ⓒ Ⓓ

**Part III**

22. See test page

### Day 2

**Part I**

1. Ⓐ Ⓑ Ⓒ Ⓓ
2. Ⓐ Ⓑ Ⓒ Ⓓ
3. Ⓐ Ⓑ Ⓒ Ⓓ
4. Ⓐ Ⓑ Ⓒ Ⓓ
5. Ⓐ Ⓑ Ⓒ Ⓓ
6. Ⓐ Ⓑ Ⓒ Ⓓ
7. Ⓐ Ⓑ Ⓒ Ⓓ
8. Ⓐ Ⓑ Ⓒ Ⓓ
9. Ⓐ Ⓑ Ⓒ Ⓓ
10. Ⓐ Ⓑ Ⓒ Ⓓ
11. Ⓐ Ⓑ Ⓒ Ⓓ
12. Ⓐ Ⓑ Ⓒ Ⓓ
13. Ⓐ Ⓑ Ⓒ Ⓓ
14. Ⓐ Ⓑ Ⓒ Ⓓ
15. Ⓐ Ⓑ Ⓒ Ⓓ
16. Ⓐ Ⓑ Ⓒ Ⓓ
17. Ⓐ Ⓑ Ⓒ Ⓓ
18. Ⓐ Ⓑ Ⓒ Ⓓ
19. Ⓐ Ⓑ Ⓒ Ⓓ
20. Ⓐ Ⓑ Ⓒ Ⓓ

**Part II**

21. See test page
22. See test page

# Mathematics Manipulatives Sheet

Regular Triangles

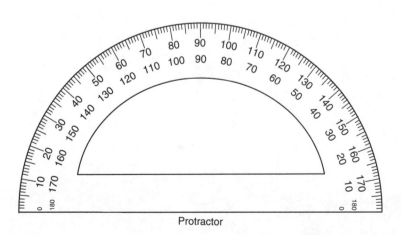

Protractor

Centimeters

Inches

Ruler

# Notes

# Notes

# Notes

# Installing REA's TestWare®

## System Requirements

Microsoft Windows XP or later. 64 MB available RAM.

## Installation

1. Insert the New Jersey ASK6 Mathematics TestWare® CD into the CD-ROM drive.

2. If the installation doesn't begin automatically, from the Start Menu, choose the RUN command. When the RUN dialog box appears, type d:\setup (where D is the letter of your CD-ROM drive) at the prompt and click OK.

3. The installation process will begin. A dialog box proposing the directory "C:\Program Files\REA\NJASK6_Math" will appear. If the name and location are suitable, click OK. If you wish to specify a different name or location, type it in and click OK.

4. Start the New Jersey ASK6 Mathematics TestWare® application by double-clicking on the icon.

REA's TestWare® is **EASY** to **LEARN AND USE**. To achieve maximum benefits, we recommend that you take a few minutes to go through the on-screen tutorial on your computer.

## Technical Support

REA's TestWare® is backed by customer and technical support. For questions about **installation or operation of your software,** contact us at:

> **Research & Education Association**
> **Phone: (732) 819-8880 (9 a.m. to 5 p. m. ET, Monday–Friday)**
> **Fax: (732) 819-8808**
> **Website: *www.rea.com***
> **E-mail: info@rea.com**

**Notes:** In order for the TestWare® to function properly, please install and run the application under the same computer administrator-level user account. Installing the TestWare® as one user and running it as another could cause file-access path conflicts.